STEP-BY-STEP GARDEN GUIDES

Martina Eva Richter

Rock Gardening

Step-by-Step Garden Guides
Rock Gardening

Martina Eva Richter

German-language edition and photographs
Gärtnern leicht und richtig Steingärten
© 1994 BLV Verlagsgesellschaft mbH, München

English-language edition
© 1995 Transedition Books, a division of Andromeda Oxford Limited, 11–13 The Vineyard, Abingdon, Oxfordshire OX14 3PX

Translation:
Andrew Shackleton/Asgard Publishing Services
Editing:
Asgard Publishing Services, Leeds
Typesetting:
Organ Graphic, Abingdon

This edition published in the UK in 1995 by Grange Books, an imprint of **Grange Books plc**, The Grange, Grange Yard, London SE1 3AG

Printed in 1995 in Dubai

ISBN 1 85627 728 3

Photographic credits
Morell 2/3, 17, 37, 61 top, 81 right, 82 left, 83, 92; Photos Horticultural frontcover, 11; Reinhard 6, 8/9, 10, 24, 34/35, 38/39, 42, 43, 51, 53 right, 53 left, 55, 56, 57, 59 top, 61 bottom, 64/65, 68/69, 73 top, 73 bottom, 74 left, 74 right, 75 right, 76 top, 76 bottom, 77 bottom, 78 left, 78 top, 78 bottom, 80, 81 left, 84, 86, 86/87, 87, 88/89, 90/91, 93, 94, 95; Reinhard-Fierfotos back cover, Sammer 12/13, 18, 28/29, 31, 33, 36, 52 left, 59 top, 77 top; Schmied 40/41, 50, 58, 72 right; Seidl 4/5, 16, 51 top, 54, 56, 57 top, 60, 72 left, 75 left, 82 right, 85 right; Stehling 7, 14/15, 19, 25, 26/27, 30, 52 right, 62/63; Strauss 22/23

CONTENTS

Designing gardens with rocks and plants

Rock gardening has become increasingly popular in recent years. Perhaps the main reason for this is that many modern gardens are small, and it's important to make the most effective possible use of this limited space. Small rock gardens are relatively easy to create, or to incorporate in an existing garden.

Rock plants, too, are enjoying ever-increasing popularity. Hill-walking holidays have given many people a taste for the lovely alpine shrubs and perennials to be found in the mountains. They return from these expeditions inspired by the beauty and harmony of the landscapes and the plants that grow there. This alone can often spur them on to create a rock garden at home.

A short history

This isn't just a modern phenomenon. The monks who created the first rock gardens in the Middle Ages were similarly inspired by the beauty and variety of the alpine flora. You can still see this when you look at monastery gardens today, especially those in the Alpine regions of Europe.

The first alpine rock garden was founded in Innsbruck in Austria by the botanist Kerner von Marilaun. He created it as an exhibition of plants for academic study.

Soon other rock gardens began to appear in Europe's parks and botanical gardens, and eventually in private gardens too. Rock-garden layouts often included accurate, almost lifelike models of mountains and peaks.

Some gardeners took this imitation to extremes, decorating their model landscapes with plaster models of mountain huts, mountaineers and even grazing cattle and sheep. Other gardeners preferred a more tasteful arrangement, such as a rock garden laid out around a garden seat, where people could sit and enjoy it at their own leisure.

The development of the landscaped rock garden was a peculiarly British phenomenon. Gardens and parks soon became filled with a vast plethora of winter-hardy alpine and rock plants, brought in from abroad by collectors and botanists.

Thanks to the ever-increasing availability of exotic species and genera, it was soon possible to create special thematic gardens. Botanical collections would include alpine gardens dedicated to the flora of particular regions such as the Hindu Kush, the Himalayas, the Caucasus or the Rockies.

Private gardens, on the other hand, were usually laid out

Spring-flowering alpines in a landscaped rock garden

according to more general aesthetic principles, combining flowers of different colours to create a magnificent display.

Among the pioneers of alpine horticulture were the authors Reginald Farrer and Walter Ingwersen, whose books and other publications on the subject provided a sound basis for the development of modern rock-garden design.

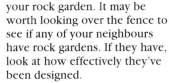

Design preliminaries

A rock garden should always be integrated into the pattern of the garden as a whole. Rocks and plants should be carefully planned to create a well-balanced landscape that doesn't look in the least artificial.

Before you even start, though, you will need to think about the lie of the land in the area where you're planning to put

your rock garden. It may be worth looking over the fence to see if any of your neighbours have rock gardens. If they have, look at how effectively they've been designed.

To build a really good rock garden, you have to know what conditions each of the plants will need, and which rocks and plants go naturally and comfortably together.

For this purpose, plants can generally be classified according to the situations where they usually grow. When you're choosing them, it's vital to consider their individual light and soil requirements.

First think about light. Will your rock garden be sunlit for most of the day, or will it be shaded?

Next — and this is just as important — what about about the chemical composition of the soil? Will the plant species you have in mind need a lime-rich, alkaline soil, or will they prefer a humous, acid soil?

The types of rock you choose will also have a noticeable effect on the soil chemistry. Most sedimentary rocks — limestone and sandstone, for instance — tend to be alkaline, and thus the surrounding soil becomes alkaline too. Granites, gneisses and slates tend towards acidity, so the soils around them will be acid in composition. So quite apart from the local topography, you'll also have to think about the pH value of the rocks you incorporate in your garden.

Every single crack in these rocks seems to be bursting with lush vegetation.

Where can I put a rock garden?

The term 'rock garden' is often used very loosely to apply to features that aren't really rock gardens at all.

A flower bed laid out with gravel or stones is definitely *not* what is meant by a rock garden. Combine some rocks or stone terracing with a suitable display of shrubs, perennials and brightly coloured annuals, and you'll be a little nearer the mark, but still a long way from the real thing.

A proper rock garden is a fully integrated feature — and to make it you must have the right kind of terrain, a good, well-thought-out garden design, some carefully chosen rocks, and a suitable selection of shrubs and alpines.

This kind of feature will have a considerable impact on the garden as a whole, at any time of the year. It works well in combination with other special features like heather gardens and ponds. An extensive lawn will blend beautifully with an alpine garden — and a peatland or wetland zone will lead nicely into a rock garden. A rock garden can also be a very effective way to use a steep slope or embankment.

A dry-stone wall can provide an extremely useful site for hanging plants; it can also be built of the same stone as the rocks in the garden, making a highly effective link between an artificial feature and a natural one.

An area of sloping land may provide the ideal site for a rock garden, but it certainly isn't the only suitable site. In a front garden, for instance, the front door makes an excellent focus for such a feature. A shady corner of the back garden can also provide some very interesting possibilities.

The important thing here is to make sure that people can come out and enjoy your feature with the minimum of effort! This is why so many rock gardens are built around a suitable seating area such as a patio or veranda. From here you can enjoy complete relaxation while still admiring all the beauties of the garden landscape.

There are some places where a rock garden simply doesn't fit — next to a vegetable patch, for example, or in the middle of a kitchen garden. But don't despair if this is the only site you have left for your rock garden. In a situation like this, the best solution is a miniature rock garden in a large trough, an old sink or some other suitable container.

A feature of this kind can even be accommodated on a balcony or patio, or just next to the front door — you don't need anything more than a few stones, one or two decorative shrubs, and a selection of attractive perennials.

Other, more adventurous sites might include a flat roof over a garage or gazebo, or possibly even the roofing over the dustbins. However, such unusual features will need very careful planning to ensure that they really work, and that they repay the trouble and imagination that will be needed in order to create them.

The important thing is to look at your garden with an imaginative yet critical eye, and to think about the solutions that will work well in your own particular circumstances. There can be very few gardens that don't have at least one place where a rock garden can be very effectively designed and incorporated.

This wall garden is covered with many different species and varieties of flower.

Choosing a site

In theory, you can include a rock feature in just about any garden. In practice, though, you'll usually have to follow a few basic rules. It's always easier, for example, to create a rock garden from scratch than to incorporate one in an existing garden.

Since a rock garden is a highly decorative feature, it should never be hidden in a corner, and is always best in a place where it will be clearly visible. It'll probably make the greatest impact on your visitors in the front garden — and it doesn't matter whether your front garden is sunny or shaded, formal or landscaped. However, some visitors — such as dogs — will definitely not be welcome, so a fence may well be useful, too.

If there are large trees in your garden, they can create a whole series of problems. Fallen petals in the summer and fallen leaves in the autumn may produce too much organic material for a rock garden to cope with, and delicate plants may be suffocated by a thick mass of rotting leaves. Leaves also encourage too much worm activity in the soil. The surface layers become too loose, so that the roots of newly planted alpines fail to connect with the deeper layers underneath. This,

in turn, makes them more liable to dry out or freeze in winter. So it's best to avoid the proximity of trees, though low-growing hedges or small flowering shrubs will make an excellent enclosure for a rock garden.

It's also important for your rock garden to be readily accessible. One ideal position is next to the main path in the front garden, where decorative stones can be seen to full effect. In a back garden, sloping ground next to a patio or garden seat makes another perfect location. Not only is the terrain ideal, but the plants are easily visible.

Sites like this are normally sunny, but they may be equally effective in the shade of a wall or fence. With time, the alpine perennials will combine with the rocks to create a beautiful, natural-looking display. You can enhance the effect still further by making sure that you use the same type of stone in the adjacent paving and in your rock garden. This will create a powerful visual link between the two elements.

A rock garden can be used to form a very tasteful boundary zone between a lawn and a bed of perennials. It will work just as well in conjunction with a heather garden, though you must be careful to make the

Back to nature — a rough limestone wall covered with natural-looking vegetation.

transition look natural. It's best if the rock garden is the more salient feature, and appears to emerge out of the heather garden. A rock garden also makes a good backdrop to a water garden — the combina-tion of two such natural-look-ing features in a small space can be very effective.

An alpine feature next to a lawn can provide the ideal habitat for many of our native orchids. Add some structure, in the form of a dry-stone wall, and you'll find that bees and other useful insects will be attracted to it in large numbers. These, in turn, will help to pollinate the various plants in your garden.

This impressively rocky landscape includes a very natural-looking stream.

When planning your garden, always pay particular attention to the needs of your family, and the use they will make of the garden.

If you have children, for example, don't put their sandpit or play area close to the rock garden. They'll always find imaginative but inappropriate places for building their sandcastles. If, on the other hand, you want to introduce them to the concept of garden design, then it's worth adding a few suitable stones to the sandpit so that they can experiment for themselves, and use their imagination without interfering with your handiwork. Later on, when the sandpit becomes redundant, it may be the ideal place for incorporating a new rock feature in an established garden layout.

A rock feature can also provide a marvellous way to make a virtue out of a necessity. The stumps of old trees, for example, can become a considerable nuisance, especially when you have to get the lawnmower round them — so why not surround them with stones, and create a small rock garden in the middle of your lawn? Take care not to spoil the effect, though. It's tempting to hide the stump under a concrete statue or vase, but these things look out of place in a rock garden. Choose something more in keeping, such as a stone or terracotta sculpture,

or a simple block of limestone or sandstone.

A rock feature invariably looks wrong next to a kitchen garden or vegetable patch, but it can provide a very suitable foil for an old-fashioned herb garden. In fact, there's no end of places where a rock garden will look exactly right.

If you can't find anywhere suitable in the garden itself, there may be a flat roof you could use for an alpine garden. In fact a rock feature of this kind is a particularly effective way of decorating *any* flat roof: on a garage, on a summer house, or even on a piece of roofing you've built to camouflage your dustbins.

Don't get carried away, though: you'll need to start by checking whether the roof is strong enough to carry the necessary weight. On average, a rock garden can weigh as much as 16–46 lb/sq ft (80–225 kg/m^2). If you're building a new structure with the express intention of incorporating a rock garden, then it can be designed to withstand this kind of pressure, but if the roof's already been built, you're going to need professional advice from an architect or a builder. Never resort to do-it-yourself methods. If the weight of the rock garden is unevenly distributed, it can cause severe damage that may prove very costly to repair.

If you're a real alpine enthusiast and you haven't a garden of your own, then you'll need to make use of every conceivable location to indulge in your hobby. Use doorsteps, landings, window-sills — in fact every space you can possibly lay your hands on.

Even a balcony can give you the opportunity to create a miniature rock garden. With a trough (or any other container) made of wood, stone or frost-proof terracotta, and a little imagination, you can build a small garden of your own. With the right materials you may be able to create a really lifelike model of an outdoor rock garden, incorporating the same wide range of plant species.

A colourful rock garden next to a lawn

Choosing soils and composts

Any soil that you use should be loosely structured and porous.

It's best to start with the surplus soil left over when you've finished laying out the garden. Break it down with a rake or a spade until you've got it to a manageable consistency, and spread it out for mixing with the other essential ingredients.

The choice and quantity of these ingredients will depend, in the first instance, on whether your soil is acid (or not), and whether it will suit the plants you have chosen.

An alkaline planting medium

It isn't very likely that you'll want to create a whole rock garden using alkaline soil; if you do, you'll be rather limited in your choice of plants.

Alkaline soil can be useful if you want to create small areas or pockets that simulate the environment in limestone or dolomite mountains; after all, these mountains are home to many attractive plants. However, a lot of these plants will also be happy with neutral or mildly acid conditions, so you only need to modify the soil for a few plants that definitely prefer it to be alkaline.

You won't often need to make the soil *very* alkaline, so it's usually enough to add some crushed limestone. For small pockets, crushed tufa is a useful addition. It's possible to use lime or crushed chalk, but they tend to leach out much more quickly and need regular replacement.

A good mix for an alkaline bed would be two parts loam, one part limestone grit and one part leaf mould or peat; you may need to add a little lime to bring the pH level up to 7.5 or just above. Use a soil-testing kit to check this.

An acid planting medium

You will, of course, need a different combination of materials in order to produce an acid soil.

We've had considerable success with a formula made up of three parts garden soil, two parts peat or bark compost, two parts crushed grit, and one part pine-needle compost. The pH value of the resulting mixture should lie between 4.5 and 5.5.

You can create a suitably acidic needle compost from a mixture of larch, spruce, fir and pine needles, though it's probably easier to buy a ready-made needle compost (designated for azaleas or peat beds) from a gardening centre.

Crushed grit is normally available from builders' merchants. The coarser gravels used for dressing drives and paths are perfectly adequate.

Soils for rock gardens can be made up of a variety of materials.

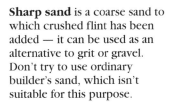

You can usually mix the soil ingredients in a wheelbarrow or some other suitable container, but large quantities can be a problem. For a layout measuring more than 220 sq ft (20 m²), or one more than 15 ft (4–5 m) square, it may be worth hiring a cement mixer.

Some other suitable additives

As well as the various ingredients we've already mentioned, there's a wide selection of soil additives that you could well find very useful for creating exactly the right soil for your rock garden:

Sharp sand is a coarse sand to which crushed flint has been added — it can be used as an alternative to grit or gravel. Don't try to use ordinary builder's sand, which isn't suitable for this purpose.

Tufa dust is produced where tufa is quarried. Tufa is a type of stone that is formed when water that contains magnesium and other minerals and salts is filtered through moss. This allows the minerals to be deposited, and they gradually accumulate to form an open, porous rock.

Tufa itself is widely used in rock gardens, and as a result tufa dust (i.e. crushed tufa) is often created as a by-product. It's ideal for adding to rock gardens to increase their porosity as well as their alkalinity.

Crushed bricks were traditionally added to rock gardens to improve drainage. Because the mixture contained mortar too, it also provided lime to sweeten the soil, either reducing its acidity or increasing its alkalinity.

Mineral aggregates such as perlite, vermiculite, arcilite and montmorillonite are increasingly used in commercial composts. They're becoming more widely available, and although they're too expensive to be used on a large scale, they can come in handy for creating odd spots in the garden where you need an open, yet moisture-retentive soil. Mineral aggregates are generally acid.

Choosing the stones: some basic geology

Natural stone is enjoying a new lease of life these days, and old quarries are being reopened to satisfy the renewed demand for building stone.

When you're choosing stones for your rock garden, you should always start by looking at the materials that are available in the general area around your home. You could perhaps take a Sunday afternoon stroll to find out what's lying around in easy reach.

But don't just limit yourself to the stones that your neighbours are using in their gardens. If, for example, you're living in a limestone area, then the brighter tints of red sandstone will look all the more exotic.

Local quarries and stone merchants may well be able to help you. You should be able to find their addresses and telephone numbers in Yellow Pages, or other local directories like Thompsons. Don't limit yourself to commercial stone merchants and quarries: it may be possible to get in touch with the storage firms who work for mining and quarrying businesses.

Left-over fragments from demolished walls, bridges and foundations may provide yet another valuable source of suitable rocks. This kind of second-hand

material is often much cheaper than freshly quarried stone — although it's worth comparing prices before you actually buy anything.

Once you've found the right stones for your purposes, you will still have the problem of getting them home. Of course, the most sensible solution is to ask the people who are selling you the stones to take care of it for you. It's not a good idea to use your own transport for anything that weighs much more than 5 cwt (250 kg).

Landscaping firms will also take on the job of installing the rocks in your garden. They usually charge by the hour, but a pre-arranged deal will normally work out cheaper in the long run. Again, you'll find the addresses and telephone numbers of landscaping in local directories — and again, it's worth shopping around to get the best deal.

This garden has been very attractively landscaped using a series of terraces of sandstone walling.

The origins of rocks

Rocks can be divided into three main groups — igneous, sedimentary and metamorphic — according to the way they were originally formed.

Igneous rocks

These rocks are formed when molten rock cools down and crystallises, a process that's been going on since the earth first began to solidify. The two main types of igneous rock are *extrusive* rocks (e.g. basalt), which are made up of very fine crystals, and *intrusive* rocks (e.g. granite), with a coarser crystalline structure.

Extrusive rocks derive from lava or magma extruded from volcanoes. If this material fails to reach the surface, it may form long, thin strata known as dykes and sills. In either case the crystals are small, so the rock tends to be all of a piece, with a uniform colour — usually between dark blue and greenish grey in the case of basalts — and no clearly defined surface features. Other extrusive rocks may be a paler grey because they are richer in quartz than the basalts.

Intrusive rocks (notably granite) are formed when molten rock cools deep in the earth's crust. Because they've cooled much more slowly than the volcanic rocks, and solidified under enormous pressure, their crystalline structure is much coarser. The three main components of granite are mica (which can be white or black),

quartz (which is glass-like) and feldspar (which can be white or pink). The perceived colour ranges from red to grey, depending how these crystals are mixed. Some granites are very coarsely grained, while others are much finer.

Granite is an extremely hard rock. Natural outcrops like the tors of Devon and Cornwall do eventually weather to produce rounded shapes, but most garden granites are quarried, giving them a harsh, angular outline. This makes them rather an unyielding material for the rock garden. Unless you have a cheap and ready supply, it's better to choose a stone that's easier to use.

Sedimentary rocks

Sedimentary rocks were formed by the accumulation of sediments on the floors of seas, lakes, rivers and plains. For rock gardeners, the two most useful categories are the sandstones and the limestones.

The sediments that make up these rocks were created either by the chemical and physical erosion of older rocks (producing, for instance, some of the elements of soil such as clay, sand, dust and loam), or from plant and animal remains. Rocks were formed as these sediments accumulated and hardened over millions of years.

These massive limestone blocks give a rock garden a beauty all its own.

Sandstones were formed by the accumulation of sand grains (quartz particles weathered out of existing rocks). These grains became cemented together to form rocks. In harder sandstones the cement consists of quartz deposited from silicic acid. Softer sandstones are bonded with calcite ($CaCO_3$) or other minerals.

Sandstones come in a panoply of colours ranging from black through brown, red, yellow, ochre and green to pure white. Among the most suitable types for rock gardens are Wealden stone and calcareous sandstones. The sandstones (and the limestones too) vary enormously in age, since they have been formed during many different epochs in the earth's history, and both groups are widespread throughout the world.

The limestones were formed mainly from the shells and other hard parts of prehistoric sea life, which broke down to form calcite. They may also contain sand or clay. Many limestone strata contain fossilised shells and imprints of early sea creatures. Mussels, snails and squid are among the modern representatives of these ancient orders of invertebrates. Their remains gradually floated down to the sea bed, where they accumulated in layers, or strata, over millions of years. Geologists can read these strata almost like a book, and palaeontologists have determined how life originated and evolved on the earth by studying fossils like these.

Ancient eroded rocks make a rock garden look much wilder and more natural.

Britain is extremely rich in limestones, but the Carboniferous limestone of central northern England and the Oolitic limestone of the Cotswolds are best for rock gardens.

Among the youngest and most useful forms of limestone is tufa. This is a soft, porous rock precipitated out of rivers and springs that have flowed through limestone strata. The colour of tufa varies from light yellow to ivory, but because it's very porous it quickly becomes covered with moss.

Metamorphic rocks

Metamorphic rocks form when existing rocks are subjected to enormous heat and pressure deep down in the earth's crust. In this way they are transformed (metamorphosed) into new types of rock.

Among the commonest representatives of this group are the crystalline quartzites and gneisses. Quartzites are metamorphosed sandstones; gneisses (metamorphosed granites) have a distinctive banded structure.

But perhaps the best-known metamorphic rocks are the slates, which derive mainly from clays. Their sheet-like structures make them an ideal roofing material, and they're also used for doorsteps, stepping stones and low dry-stone walls. They include the famous blue-grey slates of North Wales and the greener slates of the English Lake District.

Blocks of tufa usually contain natural depressions where plants can be grown to good effect.

Working with stone

The three groups of rocks can effectively be treated as two, according to their general characteristics.

Metamorphic and igneous rocks both tend to be extremely hard and dense; they are very durable, but working them usually calls for a considerable amount of effort.

Sedimentary rocks, on the other hand, tend to be less dense, which means that as a general rule they are noticeably easier to work with. There are, however, several notable exceptions in each of these groups, and each rock has its own individual characteristics.

In the end, of course, success or failure depends on having the right tools available and using the right methods. Before starting to work with these materials, it's a good idea to consult an expert such as a sculptor or stonemason, and to watch them at work.

There's no substitute for seeing how the job is actually done, except perhaps some actual, hands-on experience — which is also available if you're willing to look for it. A number of local colleges and further-education establishments offer sculpture courses, and these can be an ideal way of learning how to work with stone.

Igneous and metamorphic rocks

Igneous and metamorphic rocks are not at all widely used as rock-garden material in Britain. They're usually very hard, and they don't have the bedding planes that are such an essential element in the design of a rock garden.

Materials like granite can be used, but not, as a rule, for building the main structure of the garden. (Crushed granite fragments can be very useful for top-dressing the beds.) However, if there are no suitable limestones and sandstones available in your own particular area, it is possible to use a few igneous or metamorphic rocks as substitutes.

Basalt: Basalt is very hard and dense, and it's a rather difficult stone to work with. It usually arrives in the form of large, irregular blocks, and is suitable both as a rock for the garden itself and as a stepping stone.

You can find basalt in a wide variety of colours, including black, dark blue, greenish tones, and reddish tones — often you'll find that these colours are mixed in the same block.

Basalt occurs in Northern Ireland, the Inner Hebrides of Scotland, Central Scotland and the Welsh borders.

Granite: Granite is extremely hard, with a rough crystalline structure. It can be sawn or drilled. It is available in rounded or irregular blocks, and is ideal both for rocks and for stepping stones.

Granite comes in a wide variety of colours that range from a light blue-grey through yellowish grey and light reddish grey to red.

It is found both in Devon and Cornwall, and in the Grampian ranges of Scotland.

Gneiss: Gneiss is even denser than granite, but tends towards brittleness. It can, however, be cleaved. It's available in irregular slabs that are suitable for dry-stone walling or as rough paving stones.

Gneiss colours are generally light or dark grey, with reddish tones. This rock is generally found in the Outer Hebrides and in Northern Scotland.

Slate: Slate is hard, but less dense than gneiss, and can easily be split into thin slabs, which can then be sawn and drilled to make roofing slates. It's suitable for paving stones or flat rocks.

Slates range in colour from black to dark-blue. They occur in North Wales, the Lake District and Cornwall.

Sedimentary rocks

Coal Measures sandstones: These have a fine, even grain: they're strong and very durable, and can be cleaved and sawn. They come in regular-shaped blocks and slabs.

Their colours are mainly browns and yellows, and they are mostly found in northern England.

Old Red Sandstone: This Devonian sandstone is very durable and can be sawn. It comes in regular blocks.

As the name suggests, this rock is normally red, but it can range in colour from pink to grey. It's found in the West Midlands.

Oolitic limestone: This sandy limestone is durable, and can be sawn or split. It comes in regular or irregular blocks. The colour varies from golden to pale yellow. It is found in southern and central England.

Tufa: This rock is formed from the deposits left behind when water containing calcium or magnesium salts is filtered through moss. It is very soft and porous; plants can be grown directly in it. Tufa comes in irregular blocks, and is grey in colour. It is found in Wales.

Wealden stone: This Cretaceous sandstone is fine-grained, strong and very durable: it can be split and sawn. Wealden stone comes in regular or irregular blocks, and in a variety of soft brown and yellow colours. It's mostly found in southern England.

Westmorland stone: This water-worn limestone is traditionally the most popular rock-garden material. It can be worked, and comes in regular blocks, white or grey in colour. Westmorland stone occurs in northern England.

This slate wall has a tidy, geometric appearance.

How to place the stones

There are several things you are going to need to think about before you start.

First of all, do you mean to hire a garden specialist or land-scaping firm to transport the rocks and lay them in position for you? Or are you going to attempt the task for yourself?

It's best to draw a few sketches beforehand: these will help you to work out the best route for carrying each rock across the garden. You also need to store the rocks as close as possible to their eventual positions. And when the big day arrives, you'll need to have a good team of strong assistants on hand in order to move the rocks into place.

If possible, you should plan the whole operation for a period of fine weather. There's nothing nastier (and nothing more dangerous) than trying to carry heavy stones across a morass of slippery mud.

For the first job you'll need a flat (or round) shovel. Use it to dig out a series of shallow depressions that are the right size to accommodate each of the rocks you're going to install. Then you and your assistants can start carrying each of the stones to its chosen position.

Look at each stone carefully, and think about the safest and most effective way of moving it. Whatever method you choose — a sturdy wheelbarrow or rollers, for instance — you need

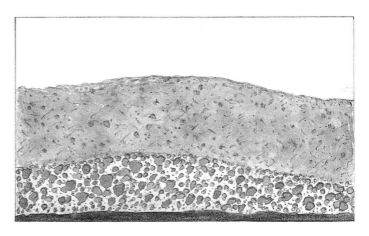

Above Provided you've installed the various layers correctly (see page 24), you can safely incorporate some larger rocks.

Right An appropriate layout made up of rocks of various sizes

to think through each individual manoeuvre very carefully beforehand.

You also need to think hard about the safety of everyone involved. For instance, try to avoid the slightest possibility that any member of your team could slip, stumble or fall. If there's anything lying around that people might trip over, then take it away to a safe distance. It's a very good idea to put down plenty of planks to provide a safe, dry path across muddy terrain (long poles could do the same job, as long as you've got enough of them, but planks are preferable).

Everyone in your team should wear strong protective gloves, sturdy work trousers (*never* shorts) and proper steel-tipped boots that will give them some protection if they are unlucky enough to drop one of the rocks on their foot (or, worse, on someone else's foot). It's surprising how many people

seem to think that wearing the right clothes and shoes is both unnecessary and uncomfortable — until they have an accident, that is.

You should already have worked out a route for each stone (see above). Normally you'll begin with the stones at the bottom of the rock garden and work gradually up to the top. However, do try to avoid the need to drag any of the stones over others that you've already laid — they could very easily slip out of position if you do. Moving them back again is usually very difficult, and calls for a tremendous amount of extra effort.

If you need to split a large rock in two, take great care to observe all the necessary safety precautions. A stone can normally be split into two or three pieces using a stonemason's hammer and chisel, but bed it in sand first: this will ensure it doesn't splinter or explode into little pieces.

The sand should be at least 2 in (5 cm) thick so as to absorb the force of the hammer. Cover the rock with plastic sheeting at the same time: this will reduce the risk of any damage caused by flying splinters. You should also wear protective gloves and goggles while you're working, to prevent the risk of any injury to your hands or your eyes.

Never, ever, use a circular stone saw or any other cutting machinery. This equipment is available from some hire shops, but it is not for the amateur. It is extremely dangerous except in the hands of highly skilled professionals.

Creating your own rocks

If you only have smallish stones available, measuring no more than 4-16 in (10-40 cm), then it's possible to create much larger rocks with them. All you will need (apart from a lot of stones) is sand, cement and a reasonable amount of clear plastic sheeting.

Dig out three to five holes in the ground, each with different dimensions. The first hole, for example, might measure 16 in (40 cm) deep by 20 in (50 cm) wide by 24 in (60 cm) long; the second hole might measure $24 \times 16 \times 20$ in ($60 \times 40 \times 50$ cm); and the third hole might be $20 \times 16 \times 28$ in ($50 \times 40 \times 70$ cm). These are only suggestions: you can, of course, dig more holes, and you can vary them as much as you like: what you're trying to do with them is to create a series of totally individual moulds, and the size will of course depend on your own particular requirements for the job in hand.

Lay ropes crosswise over the bed of each hole, and lay plastic sheeting on top of the ropes as a liner. Put your stones on the plastic sheeting, starting from the edge of each hole and working inwards until it is fully lined with stones. Then fill the middle of each hole with a mixture of five parts sand and one part cement. Check that the mixture is damp to the touch, and press it down hard with a tamper. It should fill the gaps between the stones completely, and bind them firmly together.

After three or four days these home-made rocks are ready to take out of their moulds. Lift them out together with the plastic sheeting, using the ropes that you laid underneath (you'll need at least one person to help you with this). Turn them over, carefully remove the plastic, and your rocks will be ready to use — that is, apart from a little work with a hammer and chisel to remove any excess cement from the surface.

The best stones for creating your own rocks are limestones and sandstones, although highly coloured sandstones won't give a very satisfactory result. Tufa can also be used.

Any remaining gaps in the rocks can be filled with soil and planted with suitable bedding plants. You could even leave ridges in the moulds, to create rocks with a variety of natural-looking grooves.

Plan and build a landscaped rock garden

Today's concern for the environment affects our private gardens, too. Gardeners are increasingly adopting the new ideas, and trying to create natural-looking gardens that are ecologically self-sufficient. Hence the current interest in building garden ponds, peat beds, dry meadows, woodland landscapes and, of course, rock gardens. All of them are an attempt to recreate a small piece of nature next to your own home.

The planning stage

If you decide you're going to create a natural-looking layout, this will obviously influence your choice of stones. You will need rough, unworked stones that can be integrated into the layout to create the kind of wild landscape you might find on a hillside.

Rough, uncut stones straight from the quarry are more varied in size, shape and structure than building stones that have been cut and worked to a uniform pattern. They're often better value, too, and much more varied in colour, with a marked contrast between the original open surfaces and those cut out of the stone. The end result is far more visually

exciting, producing a really powerful impression of nature in the raw.

The careful planning that goes into creating such a landscape should not be apparent in the final result. Achieving this calls for a great deal of sensitivity and imagination. It's isn't as easy as you might think to produce something that gives an impression of harmony

while at the same time looking wild and untouched.

There's a wide choice of possible locations, and most gardens will have somewhere suitable. However, the immediate surroundings should also be informal and natural-looking. A landscaped rock garden will look good, for example, next to a bed of wild perennials, a rugged pathway, a pond bank or an informal lawn. It's also much easier to integrate a rock garden into a newly laid-out garden than to incorporate it in an existing layout, especially one that is formally divided

into sections. On the other hand, a rock garden can provide the starting point for the complete replanning of an older, more formal garden. Old tree stumps and decorative branches are no more difficult to incorporate into the overall design than rocks and stones.

When looking for the best way of combining a rock landscape with the rest of your garden, you'll find no better guide than nature itself. Before deciding on your concept, see how much inspiration you can draw from the countryside around. Spend some time looking at some actual wild landscapes such as hillsides, heathlands, crags or even quarries that have been reclaimed and landscaped. Study how the rocks and stones are grouped together. A sketch-pad and a pen or pencil may come in handy at this stage — or a camera if you prefer. Use your mind's eye to try to capture some of these land-scapes, and imagine how they might look in your garden.

The most important thing is to create something you really like, which will give pleasure to you as well as to other people. Other places you might turn to for inspiration are the alpine sections of botanical gardens, rock gardens in municipal parks, or relevant pictures and designs in specialist books and magazines.

Some garden centres that specialise in alpine plants have their own rock-garden layouts, and provide lots of useful information. This will also give you a chance to find out the kinds of plants that might be suitable for a landscaped rock garden. Concentrate, if possible, on wild alpine species, and on shrubs that have been propagated by the most natural means. Cultivated perennials with large flowers in artificial-looking colours will look really out of place among a host of wild alpine species.

As well as rocks and plants, there is another natural element — water — that can be very effective indeed in a landscaped garden. Combine your rock garden with a natur-al-looking stream, and your landscape is made. A stream will look particularly good if it can be channelled into a nearby pond or marshy area, but it will also need plenty of forward planning.

This landscaped garden is made up of limestone rocks interspersed with decorative plants.

Apart from anything else, you'll need to have water and electricity supplies close at hand. A suitable water pump is essential, and you may also need to add some lights.

Atmospheric lighting can make all the difference to a water garden in the evenings, without being too obvious in the daytime. Simple garden lights or spotlights are quite adequate for this purpose, but you'll need to check that they don't dazzle any of your visitors, or your neighbours in adjacent gardens.

If you need to lay electrical cables across the garden, either for the water pump or for a power socket, then you must call in a fully qualified electrician. Don't try to do it yourself: you could be running the risk of a fatal accident.

The construction stage

Once you've planned your rock garden, you'll need to obtain the materials to build it. If you're moving into a new house (and a new garden), there may well be some extra sand, grit and topsoil left over. As long as it isn't polluted with cement or other building materials, you can use it to create your garden.

Start with a spade, and dig over the area you're going to lay out, carefully removing any weeds or roots that you find. Then use a rake to loosen up the surface soil, at the same time creating a slight rise in the middle of the site.

First you'll need a layer of gravel to provide drainage for your rock plants and stop them becoming waterlogged. Bring in several barrowfuls of coarse

gravel with a grain size of about 1-3 in (32-72 mm). Spread it out to form a layer about 8-10 in (20-25 cm) thick. If you can't get gravel, you could use a suitable crushed stone (e.g. limestone gravel) with a similar grain size.

Vary the thickness of the gravel according to your plans for the garden, creating ridges and troughs where they are needed to accommodate the rocks at a later stage.

Now it's time to bring in the topsoil. Check it's damp to the touch, and use a flat spade to

Even the smallest rock fissures can provide a suitable niche for many alpines.

spread it over the gravel to a thickness of 12–17 in (30–45 cm). Then firm it all down with the back of the spade, or a tamper. The damper the soil, the easier this job will be — so you may find it helpful to wet the whole surface with a fine water spray.

Firming down the topsoil helps bind it permanently to the drainage layer underneath. If this isn't done, the rocks will tend to shift later on as the topsoil subsides, so it's important to do the job properly. When you can walk over the soil without sinking in more than 1 in (3 cm), then you can stop tamping.

Of course, you can always make further changes to the thickness of the soil layer for your final layout.

Now, at last, you can start putting in the rocks. Take care to work out the area occupied by rocks in proportion to the area as a whole. As a rule of thumb, rocks should take up 50 per cent of the total area. Planting areas about 12–20 in (30–50 cm) wide between individual rock groups should take up about 30 per cent. The remaining 20 per cent should consist of narrow planting strips 2–4 in (5–10 cm) wide running between individual outcrops. These narrow bands should run right across the whole rock garden, linking the lower-lying planting areas with the higher ones.

The varied height of the different parts of the garden

will give the impression of a natural landscape.

Place the rocks so they look completely random at first sight. You shouldn't be able to detect any patterns unless you look really closely. In a natural landscape larger rocks are normally surrounded by groups of smaller rocks. You can imitate this by installing a larger rock with long edges in a central position, and building in small or medium-sized rocks all around it. The result will be a rounded profile that is more restful to the eye.

A spiral configuration will suit rocks of a more acid composition, such as gneiss, granite or basalt. Sedimentary rocks such as limestones and sandstones work better in a more oval

Rocks of several different shapes help to create an atmosphere of interest and variety.

pattern, or in a stepped configuration with the tallest rocks towards the centre or back of each group.

 Even in a landscaped rock garden you should avoid mixing very different types of rock. For example, the typically rounded profiles of gritstones and granites will look out of place next to limestones, with their more geometrical shapes. The resulting pattern will look unbalanced and unnatural.

Plan and build a formal rock garden

A formal rock garden is usually characterised by straight lines and regular angles — straight paths, straight walls and regularly shaped stones. In other words, nothing could provide a greater contrast to the landscaped rock garden described in the previous section.

The garden is divided into well-defined areas that relate to each other in an orderly way. It's usually orientated towards a fixed point or boundary, such as a house wall or garden fence. The rocks used in this kind of garden normally exhibit a certain unity of shape. Rough edges are filed down, and the stones are worked into similar patterns and shapes.

Formal rock gardens were a common stylistic feature of gardens attached to villas and country houses built during the early part of the 20th century. Stones were used to surround raised flower beds, sunken lawns or similar features, and these in turn were square, round or otherwise geometrical in design.

Such estates have often been preserved in their original form right down to the present day. The extensive gardens are subdivided into various sections. Kitchen garden, orchard, lawns, shrubbery and flower beds are clearly separated from each other; even within an individual section, there are clear distinctions between the various components. Despite this, however, there is an overall impression of size and unity.

Modern gardens, alas, can seldom offer such generous amounts of space, so it's less likely that a formal rock garden will offer the most appropriate solution. But if it does, then it's normally the house itself that forms the focus around which such a garden is arranged. If the rocks selected for the garden are of the same stone as the house, the end result can be very effective.

The commonest building stones used are the various types of limestone and sandstone — although granite and slate have also been used in those areas where they are readily available.

An extensive bed of wild-looking garden perennials helps to soften the otherwise harsh lines of this lovely ancient wall.

A formal rock garden should be divided off from the rest of the garden by regular paths or boundaries. This means that the best site for such a feature might be immediately in front of the house, or adjoining a raised seating area next to a main path or thoroughfare.

Again, it's a good idea to pave the path with the same stone as the rocks in the garden; this will create a feeling of unity and harmony. You can further enhance the effect by choosing paving stones with a square or rectangular shape.

Try not to mix in elements that would be more appropriate to a landscaped rock garden. Carefully shaped stones don't really match in with natural-looking features such as tree stumps, or mossy branches from dead trees.

On the other hand, formal rock gardens can look particularly attractive when they're planted out with bedding plants. These tend to spread over the adjoining paved areas, softening the strict geometrical lines and giving the garden a livelier feel.

As the most suitable plant species are sun-lovers, it's best to place the garden in a southerly or south-westerly position. The less colourful shade-loving plants tend to make a formal garden seem cold and uninviting.

The price of a formal garden is another important factor in the equation. There's a good deal of extra work involved in shaping the stones; as a result, it can cost you from three to five times as much as using the same rocks in their original unshaped form to create a landscaped garden.

The stones for a formal rock garden may cost as much as £100 or even £200 per square metre; the unworked stones for a landscaped garden might cost no more than £25, or at the most £50, for the same area.

In the end, however, your choice may quite simply depend on the amount of money you have available to spend on the project.

The construction stage

It's sometimes possible for experienced amateurs to build a landscaped garden on their own. This isn't really true of formal gardens. The skills required to cut and lay the stones in a regular pattern are well beyond what most amateurs can hope to achieve. All too often, the result of such an attempt will be an ignominious pile of broken-up stones.

To create a successful formal rock garden, you must be able to apply many different but essential rules. Stones of different sizes must be carefully arranged to form an orderly pattern. The area will need to be surrounded and subdivided by stone kerbs or low retaining walls, with a path leading through the middle to provide a sense of unity.

The construction methods are similar to those for landscaped gardens, and again it's important to have your electricity and water supplies close at hand. If the design calls for several layers of stone, one on top of the other, you'll need to think about the resulting pressure on the underlying soil. If it's too great, you may need to install some concrete foundations. It's important to add extra gravel around the individual stones.

Even the smallest rock garden can look very effective when seen at close quarters.

As well as providing additional stability, this will help with drainage. It should ensure that the soil is less liable to become waterlogged, and this in turn will help to ensure that the stones are less vulnerable to frost damage.

The planting areas will need a soil medium similar to the one specified earlier for landscaped gardens. As before, the actual area occupied by planting beds really depends on the area of the rock garden as a whole.

However, for formal gardens the rule of thumb is slightly different. Generally speaking, about 40 per cent of the area should be occupied by upright or lying stones. Open planting areas between groups of stones should take up 50 per cent of the total, and the final 10 per cent should be occupied by decorative features, such as formal rows of paving stones. Lines of paving stones 2 in (6 cm) thick and 8-16 in (20-40 cm) long also provide useful access paths to the various different planting beds.

Sloping areas need to be divided up and supported by low retaining walls or stone kerbs. The number of walls you need will depend on the difference in height between the top and bottom of the slope. For every 20 in (50 cm) of height difference, there should be one stone kerb at least 4-6 in (10-15 cm) high.

This means an area that is 5 ft (150 cm) higher at the top than at the bottom will need at least four stone kerbs. The lowest kerb should be up to 4 in (10 cm) higher than the bottom of the slope. The second should be at a level 16-24 in (40-60 cm) higher than the bottom,. The third should be 35-40 in (90-100 cm) higher, and the fourth 50-55 in (130-140 cm).

These retaining kerbs aren't just for decoration. They'll also provide stability, and above all they'll stop the soil moving down the slope when it has been loosened (by heavy rain, for instance). It's particularly important to install a kerb next to a sealed path, or when you're dividing an area of lawn.

Leave some gaps either side of each kerb which can later be filled with bedding plants. The plants aren't purely for decoration: their roots will bind together the adjacent soil layers, ensuring even greater stability.

In a formal rock garden this kind of kerbing should always be continuous. In a landscaped garden you'll want to ensure that any row of stones is well broken up; otherwise the illusion of natural informality will be completely lost.

Design and build a dry-stone wall

Dry-stone walls will be very familiar to people living in the hillier regions of Britain. Here these walls are the usual form of field boundary, as opposed to the hedges that traditionally divide lowland fields. In the past they were built with scree washed down mountain slopes by heavy rain or melting snow. The distinctive feature of dry-stone walling is the absence of cement or mortar to bind the stones together.

Dry-stone walls can be very useful in a rock garden, where they are normally used as retaining walls to support an existing bank of earth.

The planning stage

First, decide if you need foundations. For a low wall only 4–20 in (10–50 cm) high, they won't usually be necessary. But any continuous dry-stone wall more than 20 in (50 cm) high should always have foundations.

In general you should choose a type of stone you're already using in the rock garden itself, but your choice will also depend on the kind of wall you want to build. For a neat, formal wall, use stones that can be cut cleanly down to shape, such as limestones or sandstones. A few builders' merchants sell fully prepared building stones that

are ready to use. Making them, however, calls for considerable skill with a hammer and chisel: it's labour-intensive, so it's no surprise that these stones are expensive.

Recently it has become fashionable to build garden walls out of larger, more rounded stones such as granite, gneiss or gritstone. To build a dry-stone wall out of these materials you'll have to use much larger blocks, often as much as 28–55 in (70–140 cm) long.

The traditional dry-stone wall is built from rough-hewn, roughly rectangular stones. The ideal dimensions for each stone are 10–12 in (25–30 cm) long by 2–8 in (5–20 cm) high by 4–8 in (10–20 cm) wide. You can easily break up any stone that's much bigger than this with a hammer and chisel.

The construction stage

Once you have chosen and measured up the site for your wall, you'll need to level the construction area with a flat shovel. Use a taut cord to help ensure that you produce a straight line. The ground where you're going to lay the stones will need to be compacted still further with a tamper. At its base, the width of the wall should be two-fifths of its total height. So if your wall is going to be 20 in (50 cm) high, then

The strict formality of this 1950s wall is softened by the plants that have grown out from between the stones.

the base should be 8 in (20 cm) wide. The top three-fifths of the wall — in this case 12 in (30 cm) —is known as the *crown*.

Now it's time to lay the stones. Never lay more than one layer of stones at a time. Start at one end (right or left, whichever you prefer) and work right along the wall before you start to lay the second layer. Don't begin the second layer until you've finished the first, and so on.

For maximum stability the wall should be built so it leans back into the bank that it's intended to support at an angle between 5° and 10°. So if you're building a 20-in (50-cm) wall, the top should lie 2–4 in (5–10 cm), i.e. one-tenth to one-fifth of the height, behind the base of the wall. The exact angle may also be influenced by the gradient of the bank. Use a taut cord and a plumb line to ensure that you get the angle you need.

As you build the wall, make sure the stones form an overlapping pattern. Think of the face of the wall as a road map: the gaps between stones can form T-junctions, but they should never form a crossroads: 'crossroad' patterns invariably weaken the structure of the wall. There's nothing wrong about leaving a few larger gaps between the stones: they'll provide ideal niches for planting a few suitable alpines. But do make sure the soil in these gaps is properly connected to the soil behind the wall, so the plants can take root in the bank. One way of doing this is to fill all the remaining gaps between the wall and the bank with plenty of soil, pressing it down with a wooden tamper to ensure it's properly compacted.

Another way of improving the stability of a wall is to build in a series of *tie stones*. These should be much larger than the other stones in the wall. Place them at right angles to the rest, with one end buried in the bank behind. That way they'll act like dowels in a piece of furniture, bonding the two structures — the wall and the bank — together. Each layer should have at least a few tie stones in it.

Another way to liven up the appearance of a wall is by using stones of different sizes in each layer — for instance, at various points a layer may divide into two or more thinner layers. Just make sure that the main layers and the gaps between them run horizontally. If possible, the crown of the wall should be made up of single layers of larger stones: these will enable it to carry more weight.

This lovely dry-stone wall has been built from rough-hewn limestone and planted with suitable vegetation.

Buying plants

The choice of plants available these days can be bewildering, so some garden centres include a beginners' section that will give you some help in choosing the right plants for your particular needs. They may, for example, suggest plants for sunny and for shady situations, and those suitable for large, small and miniature gardens.

If you order plants through the post, send your order as soon as possible after you receive the catalogue, or you may find some more valuable species have already sold out.

A large number of British nurseries specialise in alpines, offering a wide range of exciting plants to visiting customers and through the post. Many issue informative catalogues, and all are willing to talk to you at length about your requirements.

There are a few points to watch for when choosing shrubs and perennials:

1 Are the plants really healthy? Look carefully for any signs of pest or disease infestation.

2 Are they fully mature? The size of the plant should be enough to tell you whether it's newly planted or mature. It's always worth going for an older plant with fully formed roots, even if you find that it costs a little more.

3 Are the plants free of weeds? An experienced eye can see if there are buried weed roots simply by looking at the soil surface. If you're not sure, it may be worth taking the plant out of its pot to have a look at the root ball (although the vendors won't like it).

Once you've applied these tests, you need have no qualms about buying your plants.

Do make sure, however, that each plant comes with a proper name tag listing the genus, the species and (where appropriate) the variety, so you can avoid mixing any of them up.

Different genera and species of perennial need very different amounts of space. Vigorously spreading ground-cover species like rock cresses (*Arabis*), aubrietias (*Aubrieta*) and mouse-ears (*Cerastium*) need about 3-5 plants for every square metre/yard.

Less vigorous perennials, including *Androsace*, *Armeria* and *Primula*, need 8-15 plants per square metre/yard.

Some dwarf genera and species can be planted as thickly as 20-35 per square metre/yard. This group includes many of the *Androsace* species, whitlow grasses (*Draba*) and saxifrages (*Saxifraga*).

With shrubs, space requirements will depend on the growth habit rather than on the plant genera involved. Shrubs with a particularly interesting or unusual habit should be planted as solitaries; slow-growing shrubs with a uniform growth habit should be planted in small groups of 3-5 plants.

Nurseries provide a wide selection of high-quality plants.

Successful planting

Start by putting all the plants, still in their pots, in the positions where you intend to plant them. Now take each plant in turn out of its pot to check that its roots are properly formed. Well-developed roots are an absolute must if the plant is going to thrive properly, and dwarf shrubs in particular will need plenty of care and attention as well.

Check the roots for any pests such as insect larvae. If you find an infestation, you should hold the root ball over a bucket and remove the pests with a knife or a sharp piece of wood. To prevent any recurrence, soak the roots in a weak solution of a systemic insecticide. Don't take them out again until they are saturated and no more air bubbles are visible around them. Do remember that you should always wear a pair of waterproof gloves for this job: this will avoid any risk of the solution causing damage to your skin.

Carefully remove any weeds or mosses from the soil surface, and any weed roots or other foreign bodies buried in the soil. The root balls of shrubs and perennials often contain tiny liverworts, and rootlets of other plants such as willows,

Install each plant carefully, press down gently and give it plenty of water — that way it's sure of a good start in life.

birches and alders. If you overlook these, they will quickly develop in the new soil, and will eventually choke the perennial or shrub that you planted there. A few minutes' work now could save you many hours of backbreaking labour later on.

Before you start planting out, it's a good idea to give the roots of the plant a thorough soaking. Make sure that the root ball is completely saturated. This ensures the plant won't dry out immediately after planting. (Of course there's no need to do this if you've already soaked the roots in a solution of insecticide.)

Start by planting the shrubs. Dig a hole the right size for the plant — it may be worth filling it with extra water before planting. If the roots are matted or snarled up, untangle them gently with your fingers. Press down the soil around the plant with your feet: this will help to ensure that the roots connect

properly with the soil underneath. After you've finished, be sure to give each plant a good thorough watering.

Next plant any bulbs and perennials individually, by hand, using a trowel. Press the soil down gently around each plant, and give all of them a really good watering.

When you have finished planting, add a final mulch layer of crushed chippings or gravel of the same stone as the rocks in the garden. This layer should be about 1 in (2-3 cm) thick.

Make sure that every plant is accompanied by the name tag that was supplied with it. If you think that name tags spoil the look of your plants, place them in the soil nearby, making sure that it's clear which of them refers to which plant.

General maintenance throughout the year

You'll find that a rock garden needs a lot of attention and care compared with other types of garden.

Weeding

Once your rock garden is fully laid out and planted, you'll need to begin a period of intense observation. This is the time when you need to keep careful watch for any weeds in the soil that you may perhaps have overlooked during the planting process.

Most species — especially goutweed and thistles — will probably sprout within the first three to six weeks. If they don't, you can be reasonably certain that you have them under control.

However, the same can't be said of bindweed and horsetails. These plants can sometimes lie in wait for as long as two years before sprouting and attempting to take over. The only solution is to pull out every single offending weed or root that you can find. If they reappear, you'll presumably be even more ruthless second time around.

Once you've got rid of all the perennial weeds, you'll only have the annuals to deal with. A few seedlings will invariably gain a foothold despite the mulch layer, and they should be removed immediately. Annual plants have an earlier growth cycle than most perennials: that means these weeds will have a start on the perennials, and will choke them given half a chance.

Two particular weeds have proved particularly problematic in rock gardens: hairy bittercress (*Cardamine hirsuta*) and chickweed (*Stellaria*). Both plants have a short growth cycle and spread very fast. The seeds ripen very quickly, and those of bittercress have a kind of catapult mechanism that can spread them up to a metre/yard at a time.

Topsoil imported into the garden can introduce new weeds. Remove every one on sight before it spreads to the rest of the garden. Peat is no longer used in rock gardens, but in older ones it may have introduced one or two weeds, including rushes — again, you should make sure that these are removed before they spread. Sheep sorrel (*Rumex acetosella*) is one of the worst peat weeds.

In all rock gardens you should remove all parts of annual weeds. This is because any roots left in the soil could easily introduce fungal and other diseases. Perennial weeds should also be ruthlessly rooted out.

Winter care and protection

If you've planted your rock garden in the autumn, you'll need to take particular care during the first winter. It will be important to provide protection of some kind for the more

Beauty like this can only be achieved by dedicated care.

sensitive shrubs and perennials during periods of frost. Most plants that have survived at least one growing season in the garden will be hardy enough to live through the winter without any such protection. However, this may vary considerably from one genus or species to another.

The commonest way of protecting plants is to cover them with a loose layer of spruce, fir or pine brushwood. As well as shielding the plants from frost, this also shades them from the winter sun. The sun can often kill a plant indirectly by thawing out the surface parts, which then start to develop. The problem is that the roots remain frozen, so they can't provide the necessary water. As a result the plant cells burst and the plant eventually dies of thirst.

Ironically, permanent snow cover can often be the best protection, shielding the plants from temperature variations in the air above. However, don't leave the covers on when there's no risk of frost. In very cold areas some rock-garden

 Always keep an eye on the temperature, and listen to the weather forecasts. If frost is expected, make sure you have enough protective material on hand and ready for use to cover your plants. Otherwise your more sensitive plants may easily be lost.

enthusiasts cover their gardens from late November to mid-March (depending on the location) with a fleece layer made of glass fibre that lets through air and light.

This fleece is normally used for protecting early vegetables from snow, and is generally available from garden centres. It should be anchored with stones around the edges, and should be removed from time to time so that you can check for rodent damage.

Plants are particularly vulnerable to attack from rodents if they are kept under fleece. So if there's any evidence of rodent activity, the pests should be eradicated with a suitable poison.

Spring cleaning and preparation

During the winter, while the plants are dormant, you can tidy the garden. Remove any dead leaves left over from the autumn — in fact, it's a very good idea to remove *any* dead plant material.

Straw matting provides good winter protection in very cold areas.

Where there are dead branches and seedlings, cut them back ruthlessly with a pair of pruning shears. Most gardening experts no longer believe it necessary to paint wounds on trees and shrubs.

Dried-out flower stems may well be worth leaving. They look very attractive when they're covered with frost, and they can make a rock garden seem more natural and wild. Besides that, they can sometimes provide indirect protection for your other plants, because their hollow stems provide a winter haven for some of the insects that kill off garden pests.

On the other hand, you should never leave any dead material that is soft — or any

rotting material whatsoever — because it's a breeding ground for fungal and bacterial infections. Be quite ruthless, and cut it away completely. It's always better to remove too much than too little.

Winter snow cover can sometimes compact the soil. If you find evidence of this kind of compaction, it's best to loosen the topsoil gently with a fork. Even so, be very careful not to disturb the bulbs and tubers hidden in the soil. And don't allow the soil to mix with the mulch layer on top. If the mulch layer becomes too thin, the soil will all too soon be colonised by weeds. Indeed, it may even be necessary to top up the mulch layer at this stage of the year.

There are several other useful jobs that can be done at this time. Replace or rewrite any name tags that have become difficult to read. Replace any

dead plants with new specimens. This is also a good time to make further additions to your plant collection, and to think about any modifications that you might want to make to the design and layout of your rock garden.

Summer and autumn

From mid-May onwards water will evaporate more quickly. This often means that rainfall alone can't provide enough water for the plants. If the weather turns dry, you'll need to water them intensively. Apart from weeding, this is almost certainly the most time-consuming task you'll have to do in a rock garden.

Garden sprays have proved very effective for watering rock gardens. They'll only water the ground within a specific radius, but some of them can cover an area as large as 220 sq ft (20 m²). There's a wide selection of sprays on the market, including some with a mini-computer that can be programmed to water your garden for a specified length of time. Sophisticated systems like this can be very useful when you go away on holiday, though it's still probably a good idea to ask a friend or neighbour to keep a watchful eye on the system — indeed, on your garden in general.

Summer is also the time for collecting seeds. Growing your own plants from seed is a really fascinating hobby in itself, quite apart from the rock gardening as such. And with the help of some suitable books you should be able to achieve considerable success.

You may also get the chance to exchange new plants, as well as new ideas, with other rock-gardening enthusiasts. Some gardening clubs and societies provide access to seed-exchange networks, as well as giving plenty of helpful professional advice.

As the summer draws to a close, you'll need to cut back any of the more invasive plants that are spreading too fast and beginning take over from neighbouring species.

By the autumn your garden is beginning to look rather sad and bare. It's time to plant out most of your bulb plants.

Any bulbous plants with a tendency to spread should be planted in lattice pots (like those used in ponds). This will give their roots access to the soil, but it will also stop them from spreading further than you want them to.

Mark each spot with the plant's name tag, and preferably with a small stake as well.

Then you'll know exactly where every single clump has been planted.

Finally, as the cold weather and the frosts set in, you'll need to cover up all the newly planted shrubs and perennials (see page 35).

A covering of coniferous brushwood will protect your plants in cold spells during the first winter after planting.

What to plant and where to plant it

Apart from the rocks themselves, it is the plants in a rock garden that make it so beautiful. If you choose your plants carefully, you'll be able to create a fascinating environment that produces many new and surprising displays of colours with every changing season.

If you live in an area that has a harsh climate, or one with a tendency towards long winters and late frosts, you should buy only winter-hardy plant species. You should also limit yourself to specimens that are mature enough to survive the cold. Small, soft, immature plants don't stand a chance in such a climate. However, most alpine plants are completely cold-hardy.

When you're looking at individual genera and species, start by checking their readiness to flower; it's also important to check the exact time of the flowering season in each case.

After all, it's hardly a sensible idea to choose an early-flowering species if your garden is subject to late frosts; the flower buds are likely to appear before the last frost, and then die off before they have a chance to develop. In this situation it's best to limit yourself to species that would flower while the snow is still on the ground in their own mountain habitat.

You need a full understanding of the prevailing microclimate in your garden, so that you can then choose precisely the right genera and species to suit its specific conditions and the various seasonal changes.

If at all possible, it's well worth your while buying your plants from a nursery or gardening organisation that specialises in alpine and rock plants. It's also
39
a good idea to buy pure-bred species, so that you know exactly how the plant will eventually grow.

Never be tempted to collect plants in the wild and bring them home to put in your garden. Many native wild plants — especially rare species, and most especially alpines — are protected by law, and should never be removed from their native habitat.

In any case, you aren't likely to have much success. Most alpines growing in the wild react badly to being uprooted, and will simply die or fail to grow. Precious wild plants such as edelweiss, alpenrose or gentian

are best left in their natural habitat, where everyone can enjoy them. Use them for inspiration, but never for stocking your garden.

Careful planning is essential for a really good collection of alpine

Choose the right plants, put them in the right places, give them the right care — and you can be sure of a wonderful display.

plants. This process includes drafting a detailed map of your garden that shows what you're going to buy and where you're going to plant it.

But you should start by finding out what's available. The preliminary research — leafing through collections of fascinating plant catalogues — is one of the most interesting and exciting parts of the whole process.

And don't just look for attractive species: keep an eye open for interesting leaf formations, and plants that grow in particularly interesting or unusual ways. A rock garden should contain a wide variety of patterns as well as colours.

You can, of course, propagate your own plants, whether from seed, from cuttings or by division. It's best, however, to pot the young plants for at least a year before actually planting them out. When you plant bulbs and tubers, always mark them with a stake as well as a name tag. Otherwise you could so easily plant something on top of them and stop them growing — which would be such a waste.

The best time to plant out most alpine shrubs and perennials is in the spring, between March and April. You can also plant them out in the summer or autumn, but then you'll need to water them even more generously than usual.

 Only ever bring healthy, unadulterated plants into your rock garden. A particular plant may be well worth having, but if there's the slightest sign that the roots have been contaminated with perennial weeds, then keep it well away from your garden. Otherwise you are introducing a kind of botanical Trojan horse, and the hidden weeds will eventually take over the whole garden.

Design and create a rock garden for a sunny site

The position of your rock garden is one of the most important things you have to think about at the initial planning stage.

Any position will do for a rock garden, but on the whole it's best to avoid a south-east aspect; in winter, any frozen plants in this position will be thawed out too quickly by the early morning sun, which will almost certainly kill them.

A site facing due south will often be subject to extreme heat, especially around midday in high summer: the highest surface temperatures are recorded in south-facing gardens. This, however, should not be a problem for many of the plants you'll want to grow in a rock garden. Most alpine plants are well adapted to such conditions, and are well used to coping with the high surface temperatures produced by bright sunshine in the clear mountain air.

A site facing south-west will lie in direct sunlight from early afternoon through to the evening. However, some of the surface moisture is likely to be restored during the night, and will to a certain extent be available to the plants.

Laying out the garden
In our climate even a 'sunny' site will be subject to very varying weather conditions in the course of the year. This has implications for your choice of plants, but also, just as importantly, for the soil composition that's most likely to give you successful results. It's vital to prevent your garden from becoming waterlogged during periods of prolonged rain. If the water doesn't drain away quickly, most sun-loving alpines will simply rot and die. A really good drainage system is a must for all gardens, and it has to be included at the planning and construction stage if you're going to have any hope of success.

Start by compacting the underlying soil. Then dig out a series of drainage ditches 12 in (30 cm) deep by 8 in (20 cm) wide, at intervals of 16 in (40 cm) and with a gradient of 1 in 25 to 1 in 50 (2–4 per cent). The ditches should normally slope away from the house, except when there's already a drainage system of some kind in place. Take some plastic guttering with a diameter of 4 in (10 cm) and lay this along the bottom of the ditch. Fill

this guttering with grit; you want a grain size of ½–1½ in (16–32 mm). This will then ensure that any excess water can soak away quickly.

Over the top of the whole system you should now put down several layers of gravel of different sizes; if it's a new house, you'll often find some lying around unused. The

This rock garden is on a sunny site, and has been planted with a wealth of light-hungry alpines.

such as crushed stone, fine gravel or mixed grit. The most suitable grain size is ½-1½ in (16-32 mm), but if you mix all three materials together, then ½ in (16-18 mm) will be quite enough. Press it down as you spread it over the hardcore up to a depth of between 12 in (30 cm) and 20 in (50 cm), and then compact it again when you've finished.

You can put the rocks in this layer, too. They can be anything from 8 in (20 cm) to 55 in (140 cm) long, and will often weigh as much as 3-5 cwt (150-250 kg). These upper gravel layers should provide a stable foundation for even the heaviest stones, so that you can walk on them without them ever shifting.

Lay the stones with their largest face underneath, and at a slight angle to the soil so as to improve drainage during and after heavy rain. Semi-circular rocks are highly reminiscent of an ancient Greek or Roman amphitheatre, which makes them particularly appropriate for sunny situations.

You will probably find that there are large gaps in between the rocks. These will, however, provide plenty of room for planting out lots of shrubs and perennials.

Once you've put all the rocks in place, it's time to lay the topsoil. If your garden is in a sunny position, the topsoil needs to be porous yet still capable of retaining a certain amount of moisture.

Adding carefully measured amounts of grit will help to ventilate the soil. If you also add leaf mould, or well-rotted humus, this should help the soil to retain more water without becoming too wet or even waterlogged.

Spread plenty of topsoil over all the planting areas around and between the rocks up to a depth of 12 in (30 cm). The soil needs to be deep so that the plants will quickly develop good, strong roots.

Alpine plants, in particular, will grow long roots very fast in their search for available water, and these can penetrate a considerable depth of pure grit or stone. A strong root structure is essential to prevent the plants from being washed away in a storm — a risk that's particularly significant on unprotected south-facing sites.

If you want, you can also add some attractive smaller stones between the main rocks as a form of decoration — rather like the pebbles that can often be found at the foot of mountain screes. The resulting banded patterns are not only attractive to look at, creating a visual link between the stones, but they also help to improve the general stability of the main rock groups.

bottom (or hardcore) layers should have a grain size of at least 1½ in (32 mm). The best hardcore for a sunny location is gravel or grit with a grain size of 1½-3 in (32-72 mm). Pile it up to an even depth of 16 in (40 cm), pressing it down gently to compact and shape it.

For the upper gravel layers you'll need a finer material

Planting out

Now the topsoil has been laid, it's time for the most enjoyable part of the process: planting out. Given the enormous range of plants available, it's important to think well in advance about the kinds of shrubs and perennials that you're going to choose for your garden.

One important category you should be thinking about is a group of plants known as *pioneer species*. These are plants that grow and flower vigorously, quickly colonising the garden and providing an early foretaste of the pleasures to come. In the case of perennials, choose plants whose leaves are downy or have a waxy, bluish surface. This is a sign that they are well adapted to hot, dry situations.

Among the prettiest of these pioneers (and among the easiest to grow) are lavender (*Lavandula*), catmint (*Nepeta*), stonecrop (*Sedum*) and houseleek (*Sempervivum*). A wide and varied selection of other suitable genera and species is available from the various garden centres.

Pioneer plants are fast-rooting, and quickly develop to form beautiful displays. Never plant them singly or at random. Always buy plenty of each genus or species that you choose, and always plant them in groups of between three and five at a time.

When you're choosing shrubs, have a good look at the site where you're planning to put them, and always choose species that are well suited to sunny situations. Go and look at some natural examples of shrubs growing on wild mountain slopes, and these should give you some very useful models. Among the most interesting, perhaps, are solitaries of a certain age with an irregular growth habit.

Conifers such as larch (*Larix*), spruce (*Picea*), pine (*Pinus*) or juniper (*Juniperus*) often tend towards a spreading or creeping habit. Ask specifically at your local nursery whether they have any such forms available.

This steep, rocky slope has been planted with various light-tolerant species.

Most carry several different species. These ground-covering plants are just right for a sunny rock garden. Also make a point of asking for any plants with a fault in them. They're often better value than the more perfect specimens, and look really good in a 'wild', rocky landscape.

The same applies to the many flowering shrubs. Among the most suitable for planting here are the various dwarf forms of mezereon (*Daphne mezereum*), wild rose (*Rosa*) and rowan (*Sorbus*), not to mention the small-leaved willows (*Salix*). These forms can be difficult to get hold of, and it's often a question of keeping a look out and grabbing them quickly when they become available.

The best time for planting out is between October and April, as long as the weather isn't too wet or too cold. Plants that are installed in the summer must be watered regularly and shaded from hot sun.

A sunny rock garden can also include decorative features such as dead roots, branches or pieces of bark. But don't use any pieces of wood with moss or lichen on them, since very few mosses or lichens will grow on wood that is lying in a sunny location. The same goes for moss-covered stones from shady locations: strong sunlight quickly kills off the moss, which then turns an ugly brown colour.

A sunny rock garden will look even more authentic if you lay

a suitable mulch around all the rocks and plants. Try to use a gravel made of stone similar to the rocks themselves. The continuity of colour will make the rock surfaces look wilder and more extensive than they really are.

Mulching also helps your gardening in a number of other ways. It prevents weeds from developing and colonising the planting areas, and slows down the evaporation of moisture in the soil. It also slows down the processes that would normally compact the surface soil; that, in turn, means that you don't have to rake it quite so often, with all the consequent risks to your plants. In fact, you can sometimes get away without raking it at all.

In older rock gardens the plant species should have merged, but without crowding each other.

Choose your plants carefully, plant them with care. And with a little experience, you'll soon be able to extend the flowering season from February right through to late autumn.

Perhaps the best way to achieve this is by the judicious introduction of a selection of early-flowering bulbs — for example, spring crocuses (*Crocus*), irises (*Iris*) and snowdrops (*Galanthus*) — together with some autumn-flowering species such as autumn crocuses (*Colchicum* and *Crocus*).

Some typical gardens

A rock garden on a sunny slope

Here are three examples of sunny rock gardens. Most of the plants we've chosen for them should be fairly easy to find in local nurseries or garden centres. The plant names are keyed into the pictures as

follows: bold letters and numbers refer to the circled letters (for shrubs) and numbers (for other plants) in the picture; each is followed by the number of plants recommended for the species or variety.

Requirements: a sunny, southerly aspect, enjoying full summer sunshine. Total area: 13 ft × 26 ft = 338 sq ft (4 m × 8 m = 32 m²). Rock materials: limestone or sandstone covering an area of 108 sq ft (10 m²)

This layout will suit a gently sloping site facing south or

south-west. The selected plants can be accommodated around seating areas, small hillocks or in a front garden. The rocks can also be incorporated in an existing garden layout.

The flowering season begins with the yellow blooms of the spring adonis (*Adonis vernalis*), followed in April by both gold dust (*Alyssum saxatile*) and aubrietia (*Aubrieta*).

Yellow and blue flowers predominate throughout the spring, turning the whole site into a sea of colour. The various species of pink (*Dianthus*) appear in June, their attractive leaves adorned by beautiful flowers, most of which are very fragrant.

With high summer come the typically blue flowers of the trumpet gentian (*Gentiana acaulis*). Two species of rock

rose (*Helianthemum*) vie with one another in the number of flowers they produce. *Geranium dalmaticum* forms a broad spread of pink blooms, while the loud tints of *Erodium manescavii* are visible from a considerable distance away.

Finally, in early autumn the pretty flowers of speedwell (*Veronica*), soapwort (*Saponaria ocymoides*) and the beautiful

See page 44 for an explanation of this key.

A 1 *Buddleia alternifolia*
B 3 *Prunus tenella*
C 5 *Cytisus* × *beanii*
D 3 *Salix repens*
E 3 *Abies balsamea* 'Nana'
F 1 *Chamaecyparis obtusa* 'Nana Gracilis'
G 1 *Picea glauca* 'Laurin'
H 1 *Taxus cuspidata* 'Nana'
1 3 *Adonis vernalis*
2 5 *Alyssum saxatile* 'Compactum'
3 5 *Aubrieta* 'Royal Red'
4 8 *Campanula cochleariifolia*
5 3 *Coreopsis grandiflora* 'Early Sunrise'
6 10 *Dianthus deltoides* 'Brilliant'
7 5 *Dianthus plumarius*
8 3 *Doronicum austriacum*
9 5 *Draba azoides*
10 10 *Draba bruniifolia*
11 5 *Erodium manescavii*
12 5 *Gentiana acaulis*
13 5 *Gentiana septemfida*
14 10 *Geranium dalmaticum*
15 5 *Helianthemum apenninum*
16 5 *Helianthemum nummularium*
17 3 *Iberis saxatilis*
18 5 *Lychnis viscaria*
19 3 *Oenothera missouriensis*
20 5 *Petrorhagia saxifraga*
21 10 *Potentilla neumanniana*
22 5 *Saponaria ocymoides*
23 10 *Silene shafta* 'Splendens'
24 5 *Veronica spicata* 'Erica'
25 5 *Briza media*
26 5 *Kohleria glauca*
27 3 *Poa glauca*

evening primrose (*Oenothera*) make for some lovely colour combinations.

These genera and species have been carefully chosen to provide flowers for as many months as possible. When your rock garden completes its second year, it will have produced flowers from late February right through to late November. And even after that, the clumps of bluegrass (*Poa glauca*) look particularly good in the autumn and winter, and give the garden a feeling of wildness. The butterfly bush (*Buddleia*) attracts moths when it's in flower.

This garden doesn't need much maintenance, although the pinks and rock roses will need vigorous renovation pruning from time to time.

When the hard frosts are over, however, the shrubs will need some hard pruning to encourage new growth. The dwarf Hinoki cypress (*Chamaecyparis obtusa* 'Nana Gracilis') and Japanese yew (*Taxus cuspidata* 'Nana') can be trained into natural bonsai-like forms if you carefully thin out the densest branches about three years after planting.

The other shrubs have a naturally stunted growth habit; keep them small as they grow older by pinching out the current year's shoots. The garden may look bleak in the early spring, but can be softened by planting a few early-flowering bulbs such as tulips, crocuses and irises.

The rock garden shown here can look good on its own, or combined with a heather garden or a bed of perennials. The plant selection is just as appropriate to a formal rock garden as it is in a wilder landscaped garden.

A miniature rock garden

Requirements: a sunny, southerly aspect, enjoying full summer sunshine from 10 am to 5 pm. Total area: 10 ft × 13 ft = 130 sq ft (3 m × 4 m = 12 m²). Rock materials: calcareous sandstone covering an area of 32 sq ft (3 m²).

This rock garden is suited to small areas. The use of decorative stones is particularly appropriate for a southerly site where space is limited — a small front garden, for instance, or an open courtyard. The varied coloration of the calcareous sandstone works very effectively here.

Flowering starts with the pinkish-white blooms of *Abeliophyllum distichum*, which in mild winters can appear as early as February. From the end of March yellow flowers appear above the green cushions of golden cinquefoil (*Potentilla aurea*). The white flowers of the pasque flower (*Pulsatilla vulgaris*) start to open at much the same time. Alpine asters (*Aster alpinus*) and snow-in-summer (*Cerastium tomentosum*) round off the spring very effectively.

The second flower display begins in May, when *Minuartia laricifolia* produces a carpet of tiny white blooms. Bellflowers (*Campanula*) and sea pink (*Armeria maritima*) follow soon after, and the fragrant blooms of the garland flower (*Daphne cneorum*) attract numerous insects.

The tiny white flowers of baby's breath (*Gypsophila*) appear in the summer. Golden flax (*Linum flavum*) and *Inula*

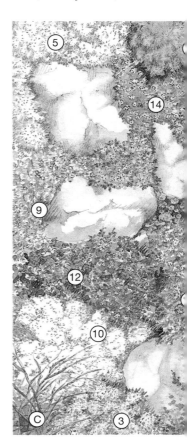

ensifolia are chock-full of yellow flowers, giving way to the varying shades of soapwort (*Saponaria*), saxifrage (*Saxifraga*) and houseleek (*Sempervivum*) as the summer goes on. Then from August into October the garden is alive with balloon flower (*Platycodon*) and germander (*Teucrium*).

During the winter months the grey fescue (*Festuca cinerea*), and the dwarf pines (*Pinus*), spruces (*Picea*) and junipers (*Juniperus*), still give some structure to the garden. Indeed, the conifers seem to make it look bigger. Meanwhile, in mild districts the winter jasmine (*Jasminum nudiflorum*) will sometimes flower as early as mid-November; its yellow blooms give a strange feeling of unreality.

Apart from some pruning this garden won't need very much maintenance, and the choice of plants means that there will be flowers for most months of the year. In the autumn the bedding plants will need to be cleared of fallen leaves so they can harden up for the winter.

The plants here are best suited to a small landscaped rock garden. The varied heights of the flowers and foliage in the garden create both an interest and an excitement that invariably compel the visitor to look more closely.

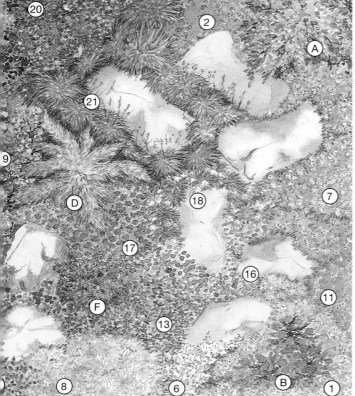

See page 44 for an explanation of this key.

A 1 *Abeliophyllum distichum*
B 3 *Daphne cneorum* 'Major'
C 1 *Jasminum nudiflorum*
D 1 *Juniperus communis* 'Hornibrookii'
E 1 *Picea abies* 'Little Gem'
F 1 *Pinus mugo* 'Mops'
1 5 *Anacyclus pyrethrum depressus*
2 5 *Armeria maritima*
3 3 *Aster alpinus* 'Albus'
4 5 *Campanula garganica*
5 5 *Cerastium tomentosum* var. columnae
6 3 *Gypsophila petraea*
7 5 *Inula ensifolia* 'Compacta'
8 5 *Leontopodium alpinum* 'Multiflorum'
9 3 *Linum flavum* 'Compactum'
10 5 *Minuartia laricifolia*
11 3 *Onosma stellulatum*
12 5 *Papaver miyabeanum* 'Takedoki'
13 3 *Platycodon grandiflorus*
14 5 *Potentilla aurea*
15 3 *Pulsatilla vulgaris* 'White Swan'
16 5 *Rosularia pallida*
17 5 *Saponaria* × *olivana*
18 3 *Saxifraga longifolia*
19 5 *Sempervivum tectorum* 'Nigrum'
20 3 *Teucrium polium aureum*
21 5 *Festuca cinerea*

A formal rock garden

Requirements: a sunny site facing south-west and enjoying bright summer sunshine from 1 pm to 8 pm. Total area of garden: 13 ft × 13 ft = 169 sq ft (4 m × 4 m = 16 m²). Rock materials: dark sandstone and sandstone chippings covering an area of 66 sq ft (5 m²).

This last example of a sunny garden is most suitable for a formal setting. Dry-stone walls of dark sandstone create just the right mood. The plants can be incorporated in square beds with square or rounded corners.

Ornamental shrubs such as maple (*Acer*), box (*Buxus*) and *Fothergilla* give the garden a Japanese feel, and this impression is heightened by the dark-coloured stone. However, instead of green mosses, flowering rock plants have been chosen for the beds that surround the shrubs. Cut box and *Fothergilla* compete with one other, although neither succeeds in stealing the limelight.

Flowering begins in March with the white-flowered rock cress (*Arabis caucasica* 'Snowball'), followed a short time later by the rich blossoms of the pink-flowered variety (*Arabis blepharophylla* 'Spring Magic'). The blue flowers of the bellflowers (*Campanula*) and small gentian (*Gentiana verna*) appear from April onwards. Mountain phlox (*Phlox subulata*) and bloody cranesbill (*Geranium sanguineum*) form loose cushions covered with flowers,

while the thorny *Acaena microphylla* creeps along the neighbouring rock crevices. The dense cushions of *Raoulia australis* form a beautiful contrast to this. The pink-and-white-flowered *Pterocephalus perennis* and the rare red- or yellow-flowered *Delphinium nudicaule* produce somewhat taller flowers.

High summer is the time for *Pterocephalus perennis*, pot marjoram (*Origanum vulgare*) and *Aster linosyris* to come into bloom. The cracks in the rocks form a comfortable home for the various saxifrages (*Saxifraga*) and thymes (*Thymus*). The thyme and marjoram provide some quite gorgeous scents. Cheddar pink (*Dianthus gratianopolitanus*), skullcap (*Scutellaria*), sea campion (*Silene uniflora*) and houseleek (*Rosularia*) thrive along the tops of the rocks.

Apart from the many plants with pretty flowers, there are various species and genera with decorative leaf patterns. These are particularly attractive in winter when covered with frost. A large blue oatgrass (*Helictotrichon*) and three clumps of feathergrass (*Stipa*) are ornamental in form, and both of them provide a splash of colour throughout the winter.

This garden won't need very much maintenance. However, the perennials have a tendency to proliferate, so every three to five years you should dig them up, divide them and replant them afresh.

SUNNY ROCK GARDENS

See page 44 for an explanation of this key.

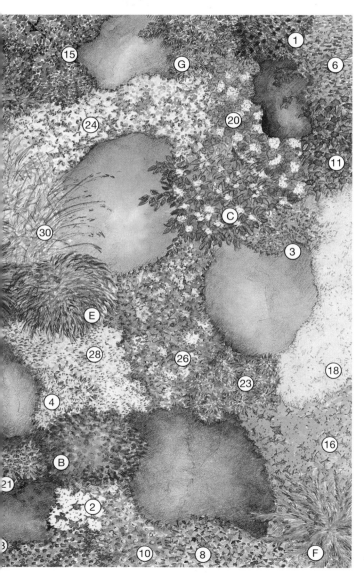

A 1 *Acer japonicum* 'Aconitifolium'
B 3 *Buxus microphylla*
C 1 *Fothergilla major*
D 1 *Salix hastata* 'Wehrhahnii'
E 1 *Chamaecyparis pisifera* 'Filifera Nana'
F 3 *Juniperus horizontalis* 'Glauca'
G 1 *Pinus cembra* 'Nana'

1 5 *Acaena microphylla* 'Copper Carpet'
2 8 *Arabis caucasica* 'Snowball'
3 3 *Arabis blepharophylla* 'Spring Magic'
4 3 *Aster linosyris*
5 5 *Campanula portenschlagiana*
6 3 *Campanula poscharskyana* 'Blue Tendril'
7 3 *Crepis aurea*
8 3 *Delphinium nudicaule*
9 5 *Dianthus gratianopolitanus* 'Splendens'
10 3 *Eriogonum umbellatum*
11 3 *Gentiana verna*
12 5 *Geranium sanguineum*
13 3 *Jasione laevis*
14 1 *Morina longifolia*
15 3 *Origanum vulgare* 'Compactum'
16 5 *Phlox subulata* 'Temiskaming'
17 3 *Pterocephalus perennis*
18 10 *Raoulia australis*
19 5 *Saxifraga paniculata*
20 5 *Saxifraga hostii*
21 3 *Scabiosa japonica var. alpina*
22 5 *Scutellaria alpina* 'Rosea'
23 5 *Scutellaria scordiifolia*
24 15 *Sedum floriferum*
25 5 *Rosularia sedoides*
26 5 *Silene uniflora* 'Plena'
27 3 *Thymus × citriodorus* 'Argenteus'
28 3 *Thymus × citriodorus* 'Golden Dwarf'
29 1 *Helictotrichon sempervirens*
30 3 *Stipa capillata*

A selection of rock-garden plants for a sunny site

Perennials

New Zealand bur
Acaena buchananii
Flowers: Aug.–Sep., brownish yellow.
Growth height: 1–2 in (2–5 cm).
Soil: loosely structured, with plenty of humus.
Propagation: seed or cuttings.
Comments: this vigorous creeper is undemanding, and excellent as an edge plant. However, it is best to site it well away from weaker-growing plants, as it will crowd them out. *A. microphylla* 'Copper Carpet' is also suitable.

Mount Atlas daisy
Anacyclus pyrethrum depressus
Flowers: May–Jun., white above, red beneath.
Growth height: 4–6 in (10–15 cm).
Soil: loosely structured.
Propagation: seed.
Comments: this plant is undemanding but not very long-lived; it forms loosely radiating leaf patterns.

Sea pink, thrift
Armeria maritima
Flowers: May–Jun., pink, red and white.
Growth height: 2 in (5 cm).

Soil: loosely structured.
Propagation: seed or division.
Comments: this is an undemanding plant, but does need to be divided and replanted every 3–4 years. Its grass-like forms develop into thick clumps.

Gold dust
Alyssum saxatile
Flower colour: yellow.

Growth height: 6–8 in (15–20 cm).
Soil: gravelly.
Propagation: seed or cuttings.
Comments: this undemanding, vigorous, early-flowering perennial is very good for planting with aubrietia or rock cress. It should be pruned back after flowering to prevent premature ageing. The woody stems bear green stalks with greenish-white leaves and golden-yellow flowers.

A beautiful clump of sea pinks (Armeria maritima) in front of a limestone rock

Golden aster
Aster linosyris
Flowers: Aug.-Sep., golden yellow.
Growth height: 12-16 in (30-40 cm).
Soil: loosely structured with plenty of gravel.
Propagation: seed or division.
Comments: golden aster is an undemanding plant with attractive autumn colouring and loosely creeping shoots.

Aubrietia
Aubrieta deltoidea
Flowers: Apr.-May, bluish, violet and reddish, occasionally white.
Growth height: 2-5 in (5-12 cm).
Soil: loosely structured.
Propagation: seed or cuttings.
Comments: this perennial is mostly grown in rock gardens. It looks highly attractive next to rock cress and gold dust, but

Aubrietia (Aubrieta) and gold dust (Alyssum saxatile) make a really lovely combination.

Campanula poscharskyana is among the most vigorous of the summer-flowering perennials.

does have a tendency to proliferate, so you should always prune it back after flowering to keep the growth compact. Its long, mat-forming shoots make an excellent covering for rocks and walls.

Tussock bellflower
Campanula carpatica
Flowers: May-Aug., blue and white.
Growth height: 3-6 in (8-15 cm).
Soil: gravelly.
Propagation: seed or cuttings.
Comments: this is an undemanding ground-cover plant with a strong tendency to spread. Tussock bellflower also grows well in rock crevices;it is clump-forming, with rather long flower stems.

Gargano bellflower
Campanula garganica
Flowers: May-Jun., white and various blue tints.
Growth height: 3-4 in (8-10 cm).
Soil: gravelly.
Propagation: seed, cuttings or division.
Other comments: this vigorous ground-cover plant forms dense clumps. Gargano bellflower looks good next to maiden pinks. If you remove the seedheads after the first flowering, this will stimulate further flowering.

Campanula poscharskyana
Flowers: May-Oct., varied tints from blue through to white.

51

Left *The lovely flowers of the maiden pink (*Dianthus deltoides*) spread out surprisingly quickly.*

Right *Alpine thistles (*Carlina acaulis*) should never be picked in the wild because they are a protected species.*

Growth height: 3-6 in (8-15 cm).
Soil: loosely structured.
Propagation: seed or division.
Comments: a vigorous ground-cover plant that spreads widely over rocks and shrubs, and bears large flowers. Prune back wilted flower shoots to encourage strong growth. This plant is particularly attractive in rock crevices, or as ground cover for larger areas.

Alpine thistle
Carlina acaulis
Flowers: Aug.-Oct., silvery white.
Growth height: 4-8 in (10-20 cm).
Soil: gravelly.

Propagation: seed.
Comments: the flowers of this ornamental thistle respond quickly to increased humidity by closing their petals. The alpine thistle forms a very effective link plant between rock and heather gardens, producing prickly leaves in dense rosettes, each bearing an attractive flower.

Yellow fumitory
Corydalis lutea
Flowers: May-Sep., golden yellow.
Growth height: 8-16 in (20-40 cm).
Soil: loosely structured.
Propagation: seed.
Comments: the yellow fumitory is undemanding, and spreads vigorously to form dense, green clumps with erect racemes of attractive flowers.

Maiden pink
Dianthus deltoides
Flowers: Jun.-Aug., white and various red tints.

Growth height: 4-6 in (10-15 cm).
Soil: loosely structured.
Propagation: seed or cuttings.
Comments: the maiden pink is a fairly undemanding plant that is often self-seeding; it forms dense, mat-like cushions of leaves.

Yellow whitlow grass
Draba aizoides
Flowers: Mar.-Apr., bright yellow.
Growth height: 2-3 in (5-8 cm).
Soil: gravelly.
Propagation: seed, cuttings or division.
Comments: this undemanding plant is especially attractive in rock crevices; its leaf rosettes form dense ground cover.

Mountain avens
Dryas octopetala
Flowers: May-Jun., white.
Growth height: 1-3 in (3-8 cm).
Soil: gravelly.

Propagation: seed or cuttings.
Comments: an undemanding plant that is very suitable for rocks and edges; its leaves are formed on creeping woody stems.

Erodium manescavii
Flowers: Jun.–Sep., red.
Growth height: 12–20 in (30–50 cm).
Soil: gravelly.
Propagation: seed.
Comments: this plant is undemanding; very pretty when in flower, and looks good in small groups; it forms dense clumps of fern-like leaves.

Erodium petraeum
Flowers: May–Aug., pink.
Growth height: 4–5 in (10–12 cm).
Soil: gravelly, with plenty of humus.
Propagation: cuttings.
Comments: protect this plant with brushwood during the first winter after planting. It is particularly attractive in rock crevices, displaying dense clumps of greyish-green, fern-like leaves.

Euphorbia myrsinites
Flowers: Apr.–May, yellow.
Growth height: 6–10 in (15–25 cm).
Soil: gravelly.
Propagation: seed or cuttings.
Comments: this plant creeps prettily over rocks and other surfaces, and takes about three years to achieve its full glory; it possesses cylindrical shoots bearing pointed, fleshy evergreen leaves.

Willow gentian
Gentiana asclepiadea
Flowers: Jul.–Sep., blue, occasionally pink or white.
Growth height: 24–39 in (60–100 cm).
Soil: gravelly with plenty of humus.
Propagation: seed.
Comments: the willow gentian is an imposing plant that looks especially attractive next to shrubs or in front of large rocks; it has loose clumps of leafy stems crowned with bell-like flowers.

Stemless gentian
Gentiana dinarica
Flowers: Apr.–Jun., blue, occasionally white.
Growth height: 2–4 in (5–10 cm).
Soil: gravelly with some loam.
Propagation: seed, cuttings or division.
Comments: when in flower, stemless gentian is one of the most beautiful alpines. It looks particularly good when it is planted in groups between rock crevices. Its leaf clusters lie close to the ground.

Left *Mountain avens (*Dryas octopetala*) is one of the prettiest flowers to be found in any rock garden.*

Right *Willow gentian (*Gentiana asclepiadea*) forms thick clumps with the passage of time.*

Summer gentian
Gentiana septemfida
Flowers: Jun.–Aug., light blue.
Growth height: 6–10 in
(15–25 cm).
Soil: gravelly with plenty of
humus.
Propagation: seed; division
occasionally possible.
Comments: summer gentian
colonises narrow rock crevices
very effectively; each of the
leafy, upright shoots bears up
to seven flowers.

Geranium dalmaticum
Flowers: Jun.–Sep., red, pink,
occasionally white.
Growth height: 5–7 in
(12–18 cm).
Soil: gravelly with a certain
amount of loam.

The bloody cranesbill (Geranium sanguineum) is a valuable native perennial.

Propagation: cuttings or
division.
Comments: *Geranium dalmaticum* has a long flowering
period, with a reddish colouring
in autumn; its creeping shoots
form dense clusters.

Bloody cranesbill
Geranium sanguineum
Flowers: May–Sep., red, pink,
occasionally white.
Growth height: 6–12 in
(15–30 cm).
Soil: plenty of humus.
Propagation: root cuttings or
seed.
Comments: this attractive and
undemanding plant has a long
flowering period; its creeping
rhizomes develop loose, leafy
shoots.

Baby's breath
Gypsophila repens
Flowers: Jun.–Jul., pink and
white.

Growth height: 3–5 in
(8–12 cm).
Soil: gravelly.
Propagation: seed.
Comments: this vigorous and
undemanding plant is very
effective in vertical rock
crevices; it forms thick clumps,
with flowers borne on long,
arching shoots.

Rock rose
*Helianthemum nummu-
larium*
Flowers: May–Aug., yellow.
Growth height: 2–4 in
(5–10 cm).
Soil: gravelly with a little
humus.
Propagation: seed or cuttings.
Comments: the rock rose is a
particularly beautiful wild
perennial that makes good
ground cover. It is a vigorous
and undemanding plant, ideal
for the rock garden.

Candytuft
Iberis sempervirens
Flowers: Apr.–Jun., white.
Growth height: 8–18 in
(20–45 cm).
Soil: loosely structured.
Propagation: seed or cuttings.
Comments: candytuft is an
evergreen; prune it back vigor-
ously after flowering to create
dense, attractive bushes.

Inula ensifolia
'Compacta'
Flowers: Jul.–Sep., yellow.
Growth height: 6–10 in
(15–25 cm).
Soil: gravelly.
Propagation: seed.

Comments: *Inula ensifolia* 'Compacta' is an ideal plant for use as ground cover. Plant it in well-dispersed groups; it will form dense clumps, with long shoots covered in numerous lance-shaped leaves.

Edelweiss
Leontopodium alpinum
Flowers: Jun.–Sep., white.
Growth height: 2–6 in (6–15 cm).
Soil: gravelly.
Propagation: seed or division.
Comments: the famous edelweiss is probably the best-known of all alpine plants. Lift, divide and replant it every 3–5 years; it is particularly attractive in narrow crevices, where it will form dense clumps of silvery-green leaves.

Golden flax
Linum flavum
Flowers: Jul.–Sep., yellow.
Growth height: 4–14 in (10–35 cm).
Soil: loosely structured.
Propagation: seed or cuttings.
Comments: golden flax is an undemanding plant with terminal flowers that looks good in front of dark-coloured conifers. Prune it back after flowering to stimulate vigorous reflowering in September.

Alpine catchfly
Lychnis alpina
Flowers: May–Jun., red and white.
Growth height: 3–6 in (8–15 cm).
Soil: gravelly.

Edelweiss (Leontopodium alpinum) is the classic alpine plant.

Propagation: seed.
Comments: protect this plant with brushwood during the first winter after planting; it forms a mat, and is suitable for narrow rock crevices.

Minuartia laricifolia
Flowers: May–Jul., white.
Growth height: 2–4 in (5–10 cm).
Soil: loosely structured.

Propagation: seed, cuttings or division.
Comments: *Minuartia laricifolia* is a creeping ground-cover plant that forms broad mats. This plant is particularly attractive next to maiden pinks or rock roses.

Left *The evening primrose is remarkable for its large yellow flowers*

Right *The Iceland poppy is a vigorous summer-flowering perennial.*

Catmint
Nepeta × faassenii
Flowers: May–Nov., blue.
Growth height: 8-14 in
(20-35 cm).
Soil: loosely structured.
Propagation: cuttings or division.
Comments: an attractive flowering perennial; prune vigorously after flowering to stimulate new growth and second flowering; has attractive blue-green leaves and shoots.

Creeping evening primrose
Oenothera missouriensis
Flowers: Jul.–Oct., yellow.

Growth height: 6-10 in
(15-25 cm).
Soil: gravelly.
Propagation: seed or cuttings.
Comments: valuable summer-flowering perennial with large yellow flowers and long shoots that hang down over the rocks.

Iceland poppy
Papaver nudicaule
Flowers: Apr.–Jul., white, red and yellow.
Growth height: 6-10 in
(15-25 cm).
Soil: loosely structured.
Propagation: seed.
Comments: normally only biennial, but lives longer if seedheads are removed immediately after flowering; self-seeds spontaneously; good for land-scaped gardens; large, brightly coloured flowers.

Tunic flower
Petrorhagia saxifraga
Flowers: Jun.–Sep., pink, white and red.
Growth height: 6-10 in
(15-25 cm).
Soil: gravelly.
Propagation: seed.
Comments: an attractive plant in even the smallest of crevices; prune back vigorously after flowering to stimulate second flowering in the autumn; forms thick clumps and long, branching shoots with terminal flowers.

Mountain phlox
Phlox subulata
Flowers: Apr.–Jun., pink, white, red and various blue tints; tend to be highly variable.
Growth height: 2-6 in
(5-15 cm).

Soil: loosely structured.
Propagation: cuttings.
Comments: plant in rock crevices in small groups made up of different-coloured flowers; lift, divide and replant it every 3-5 years.

Balloon flower
Platycodon grandiflorus
Flowers: Jul.–Sep., blue, occasionally pink and red.
Growth height: 10-16 in (25-40 cm).
Soil: gravelly with plenty of humus.
Propagation: seed or cuttings.
Comments: attractive when planted in groups in front of taller shrubs; forms dense clumps with upright shoots; goes well with mountain avens or *Minuartia laricifolia*.

Golden cinquefoil
Potentilla aurea
Flowers: Apr.–May, yellow.
Growth height: 3-5 in (8-12 cm).
Soil: gravelly.
Propagation: seed or cuttings.
Comments: the golden cinquefoil forms broad, deep-green mats that are covered with glorious yellow flowers; it should be cut back vigorously after flowering so as to encourage new growth.

Above *Golden cinquefoil (*Potentilla aurea) *is one of the early-flowering alpines.*

Below *Mountain phlox (*Phlox subulata) *is noted for its rich carpet of flowers.*

Drumstick primrose
Primula denticulata
Flowers: Apr., red, violet, pink and white tints.
Growth height: 10-14 in (25-35 cm).
Soil: soil with plenty of humus.
Propagation: seed or root cuttings.

Comments: when in flower, the drumstick primrose looks really good in groups, but in summer the fleshy leaves look rather unattractive. It bears spherical flowers on long stems growing out of dense leaf rosettes; plant it at least 12 in (30 cm) away from other plants.

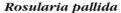

Auricula
Primula × pubescens
Flowers: Apr.-Jun., red, violet, yellow and white tints.
Growth height: 5-8 in (12-20 cm).
Soil: plenty of humus.
Propagation: seed, cuttings or division.
Comments: the flowers of the auriculas grow out of thick clumps of fleshy leaves. As older plants tend to form long shoots growing out of the soil, it's best to lift, divide and replant them every 3-5 years. Auriculas are a favourite group of collector's plants, with many different varieties available.

Pterocephalus perennis
Flowers: Jul.-Aug., pink.
Growth height: 5-6 in (12-16 cm).
Soil: gravelly.
Propagation: seed or cuttings.

Comments: *Pterocephalus perennis* provides a pleasant contrast to the darker-coloured alpines, with its low, dense mats of greyish-green leaves. Plant it in narrow crevices, and protect it with brushwood during the first winter.

Pasque flower
Pulsatilla vulgaris
Flowers: Apr.-Jun., mauve, with red, violet, white and pink forms.
Growth height: 10-14 in (25-35 cm).
Soil: gravelly.
Propagation: seed.
Comments: the pasque flower develops thick clumps of leaves, and bears attractive flowers on long stalks, followed later by pretty seedheads; it is a favourite collector's plant, with many varieties available in a host of different colours.

Rosularia pallida
Flowers: Jun.-Aug., white.
Growth height: 3-6 in (8-15 cm).
Soil: gravelly.
Propagation: division or rosette cuttings.
Comments: *Rosularia pallida* is a small ornamental perennial for planting in narrow crevices; it goes well with houseleek or saxifrage. It is highly tolerant of dryness, and develops dense mats of small, fleshy leaf rosettes.

Saponaria ocymoides
Flowers: Jun.-Sep., red and pink.
Growth height: 6-10 in (15-25 cm).
Soil: gravelly.
Propagation: seed or cuttings.
Comments: this attractive alpine is ideal for edges and good for wall crevices; a species of soapwort that forms a dense mat of overhanging shoots; it goes well with candy-tuft or rock cress.

Saxifrages
Saxifraga
This is a large genus of mainly mountain-dwelling plants, with many species and varieties that are ideally suited to rock gardens. Just a few examples are given opposite:

*The pasque flower (*Pulsatilla vulgaris*) is a protected species in the wild. There are many varieties, all of which thrive in poor soils.*

Saxifraga longifolia

Flowers: May–Jul., white.
Growth height: 10-24 in (25-60 cm).
Soil: gravelly.
Propagation: seed.
Comments: *Saxifraga longifolia* is a highly conspicuous perennial with a single rosette that becomes plate-sized in older plants. After a period of five to eight years it puts out a single cylindrical flower panicle. Individual flowers bloom from the bottom upwards; the plant will die off completely after flowering, but it seeds profusely.

Saxifraga paniculata

Flowers: May–Jul., white, occasionally with yellow and reddish tints.
Growth height: 3-6 in (8-15 cm).
Soil: gravelly.
Propagation: seed, cuttings or division.
Comments: a very attractive plant, made up of numerous tiny rosettes of lime-encrusted leaves that grow together to form a single, densely matted rosette. *Saxifraga paniculata* combines beautifully with red-leaved houseleek and wallpepper in narrow rock or wall crevices.

Saxifraga sancta

Flowers: Mar.–May, yellow.
Growth height: 2-3 in (6-8 cm).
Soil: gravelly.
Propagation: cuttings or division.

Comments: *Saxifraga sancta*, with its small mats of dark-green, needle-like leaves, looks very attractive even without any flowers. However, you will find that it tends to need extra moisture at the height of the summer. The plant is ideally suited to gardens with tufa stones, and is a valuable collector's plant.

Above Saponaria ocymoides tumbles over the top of a wall.

Below Wallpepper is one of the least demanding of all alpines.

Wallpepper, white stonecrop

Sedum alba
Flowers: May–Jul., white to pink.

Growth height: 1-2 in (3-5 cm).
Soil: loosely structured.
Propagation: cuttings or division.
Comments: an attractive yet undemanding ground-cover plant with round, fleshy leaves, the wallpepper is best suited to hot, dry situations. The leaf rosettes turn a beautiful bright red in autumn. However, the plant does tend to spread and proliferate, so that with time it can become something of a nuisance.

Common houseleek
Sempervivum tectorum
Flowers: Jun.-Aug., reddish, yellow and white tints.
Growth height: 3-12 in (8-30 cm).
Soil: gravelly.

Propagation: rosette cuttings or seed.
Comments: the common houseleek belongs to one of the most popular alpine genera. Its leaf rosettes vary enormously in both colour and pattern. This is an undemanding plant that is very attractive in narrow crevices.

Sea campion
Silene uniflora
Flowers: Jun.-Aug., white and pink.
Growth height: 4-6 in (10-15 cm).
Soil: loosely structured.
Propagation: seed or cuttings.
Comments: an undemanding plant that spreads out into extensive mats. Sea campion looks attractive in wall crevices, and goes well with rock cress and maiden pink in front of dwarf conifers.

Silene shafta 'Splendens'
Flowers: Jul.-Aug., red.
Growth height: 3-5 in (8-12 cm).
Soil: gravelly.
Propagation: seed.
Comments: this undemanding gap-filler looks particularly attractive in small groups next to grasses. It forms dense clumps, with flowers on long, thin stems.

All campions (Silene species) grow vigorously and produce flowers in profusion.

Grasses

Quaking grass
Briza media
Flowers: May-Jun., whitish.
Growth height: 12-16 in
(30-40 cm).
Soil: loosely structured.
Propagation: seed or division.
Comments: quaking grass is a
vigorous wild grass species best
suited to larger sites. It forms
greenish clumps and loose
panicles of small, heart-shaped
flowers. It is best to cut it back
immediately after flowering so
as to prevent excessive self-
seeding.

Grey fescue
Festuca cinerea
Flowers: May-Jul., yellowish
to white.
Growth height: 10-14 in
(25-35 cm).
Soil: loosely structured.
Propagation: seed or division.
Comments: grey fescue is an
undemanding ornamental grass
suitable for larger sites. It forms
grey clumps tinged with blue.
Lift, divide and replant each
clump every 3-5 years to stop
die-back in the centre; it's best
to remove the seedheads after
flowering.

Feather grass
Stipa capillata
Flowers: Jul.-Oct., whitish.
Growth height: 20-35 in
(50-90 cm).
Soil: loosely structured.
Propagation: seed.

Above *Quaking grass (*Briza media*)
looks really good in a landscaped
rock garden.*

Left *A feather grass (*Stipa*) in flower
makes a wonderfully wild display.*

Comments: vigorous ornamental grass with pretty flower
panicles; good for hot, sunny
locations; attractive in front of
conifers; seedheads retain their
beauty in winter.

61

Design and create a rock garden for a shaded site

Many experts will tell you that a rock garden on a shaded site has no hope of success.

It is, admittedly, true that gardeners have often tried it and failed. However, recent attempts to imitate nature in gardens have shown that a rock garden can indeed be attractive and successful even in the shade.

Different kinds of shade

If you look carefully at a whole selection of shaded sites, you'll quickly realise there are many different patterns of shade. Fortunately, however, we need only make a simple distinction between *permanent* and *variable* shade patterns.

Permanent shade normally occurs where houses, high walls or other structures prevent the sun from entering a particular area. The light level is subdued throughout the year, and there's always a well-defined shadow.

You can measure the actual light intensity in a particular location with a light meter; an ordinary meter of the type used by photographers is perfectly adequate. The main unit of measurement is the lux, and if the light intensity measures less than 500 lux, the site is clearly unsuitable for an alpine garden.

If, on the other hand, you find that the light intensity measures more than 1,500 lux, then perhaps you're in with more than a chance.

Some buildings and other structures can also create variable shade patterns. Some walls, for example, cast comparatively little shade, and as a result the light intensity nearby will be correspondingly higher all year round.

Variable shade is usually created by less rigid objects, such as trees. Their shadows move with the sun, or when the wind catches them, which means that the areas they shade are intermittently lit by the sun.

Preliminary research

If you're planning to create a rock garden on a shaded site, then you'll need to go and have a look at some correspondingly shaded locations in the wild, and to study what actually grows there.

Perhaps the best lowland sites are abandoned quarries that have been allowed to go wild.

Apart from grasses, the first plants to appear in these locations will be fast-growing shrubs such as hazel (*Corylus*) and willow (*Salix*). These plants soon put some of the rock surfaces in the shade, and the vegetation growing here will be of special interest. The crevices are colonised by

A shaded rock garden can bring shrubs and perennials together in delightful harmony.

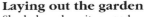
mossy saxifrages, rock-dwelling ferns and other arractive rock plants. Low-growing shrubs such as bilberry (*Vaccinium myrtillus*), the closely related *V. myriophyllum* and heather (*Calluna vulgaris*) thrive around the more acid rocks such as gneiss, granite and some sandstones.

The best upland sites to look at are rocky areas below cliffs, or to the north of high ground. Apart from grasses, ferns and a whole variety of mosses and lichens, you'll find an extensive range of shrubs and perennials.

The crowberry (*Empetrum nigrum*) and the bearberry (*Arctostaphylos uva-ursi*) occur mainly on limestone; their fine branches will often cover an extensive area of rock. Mosses and lichens grow mainly on rocks and among the vegetation, and they are always a clear indicator of the amount of available moisture.

Laying out the garden

Shaded garden sites need appreciably more moisture than sunny ones, though if possible you should still avoid any risk of waterlogging. However, it isn't normally necessary to install a drainage system underneath such sites.

You should first rake over the soil, and then mould it into the shape you want and press it down gently to compact it before adding the hardcore.

The main purpose of raking the soil is to make sure there are no weed roots left in it. If you leave the slightest trace of any perennial weeds such as horsetails, goutweed, couch grass, bindweed or thistles, then these will be virtually impossible to eradicate later on. If you don't pay enough attention at this early stage you may well be sowing the seeds of failure. In due course you'll find that you're spending all your time trying to get rid of these ineradicable weeds, and you'll soon lose any enthusiasm for the project.

Next you should put down a layer of hardcore to a maximum depth of 20 in (50 cm). The material we recommend is basalt or limestone gravel with

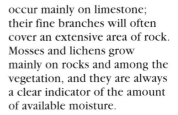

an average grain size of 1.3 in (32 mm). However, if you mix in some rougher gravel varying in size from 1.3 in (32 mm) to 2.8 in (72 mm), you can allow up to 30 per cent of sand and soil in the mix.

The organic component helps to bind the hardcore as you start to compact it. Do this at the end of the process, using the back of a flat spade. It's worth wetting the hardcore before you start — just sprinkle it with a little water from an ordinary watering can. This will help to speed up the compaction process.

Now add a second layer on top of the hardcore, this time using a mixture of crushed stone, fine gravel, mixed grit and weed-free topsoil. The soil must contain at least some loam and humus, while the inorganic components should have a grain size of ½–1½ in (16–32 mm).

The final mixture should contain the same amount of soil as the rest of the ingredients put together. This second layer needs to be about 16 in (40 cm) thick. Again, you will find that the mixture compacts more quickly and evenly if you wet it slightly.

The next stage is to take a flat spade and dig out some holes, ready to receive the rocks. These need to be arranged in a different way from those on a sunny site: build them into small pyramids of between three and seven stones. This produces a layout with more

variety in height, and in the size of the gaps between the rocks; generally these should be smaller than they would be in a sunny garden

Lay the rocks at a slight angle so that the water collects in a series of small depressions. These depressions can then act as miniature water reservoirs. This is a feature quite commonly found on mountain slopes, where depressions of this kind also retain snow in the winter. As a result the snow remains here longer during the spring thaw, keeping the temperature lower than it is elsewhere. This is beneficial not only in providing higher humidity, but because a shaded location also benefits from lower average temperatures.

Once you've put the rocks in place, it's time to incorporate other natural features in between them, such as large tree stumps (complete with roots). Old oak or beech stumps are particularly effective. Take a walk through the woods, and see what kinds of natural decoration you can find — but before you dig anything up, make sure you have the permission of the landowner or responsible authority.

Depending on the size of the rock garden, any tree roots should be between 20 in (50 cm) and 5 ft (150 cm) long. Always place your stumps in the garden so they look as if they had actually grown there. It's important to avoid anything that looks unnatural.

When you come to laying the topsoil, you may already have some suitable humus-rich, weed-free soil available. If so, this can form the basis of your planting medium. Bear in mind that shaded sites need plenty of humus, but that the shade also encourages the formation of humus.

The most suitable mixture is a combination of bark compost, finely crushed grit and soil. Leaf composts can also be used, but peat is now frowned on for ecological reasons.

The final mixture should contain about 70 per cent organic material. For smaller areas of up to 54 sq ft (5 m²) you can easily mix the soil in a wheelbarrow. For areas larger than 215 sq ft (20 m²) you'll find it much easier to use a cement mixer.

Spread the topsoil evenly to a depth of 8–10 in (20–25 cm), pressing it down gently when you've finished.

Planting out
Now, at last, you can plant out your first shrubs and alpines. The best time to do this is either between mid-March and the end of May, or between the beginning of September and mid-November.

As the planting areas between the stones and stumps are narrower than in a sunny rock garden, you should place the plants side by side rather than in groups, using between three and five specimens of each species. Again, make sure you don't plant any species singly, or mix the species up.

The flowering season begins early, even on a shaded site.

Anemones (*Anemone*), liverleaf (*Hepatica*) and *Corydalis* will flower as early as March.

Late spring is the time for one of our most valuable shade-loving perennials: the lady's slipper orchid (*Cypripedium calceolus*), which flowers around Whitsuntide, is one of the rarest of our native orchids. The primroses (*Primula*) are then followed in succession by a variety of different saxifrages (*Saxifraga*).

Nowadays, thanks to modern commercial propagation methods, there is a wide choice of rare and lovely plants available that can be successfully incorporated in a shaded rock garden. And quite apart from the many beautiful flowers, there are many suitable plants that possess highly decorative leaf patterns.

Mosses and lichens
The rocks provide the ideal site for various naturally occurring mosses and lichens, which will make your garden look even more natural.

Moss-covered rocks in turn provide an environment where some perennials will seed, with the result that they can colonise the actual rock surfaces.

Provided there is sufficient humidity, the moss and lichen should be able to grow naturally over the rocks without your having to do anything.

If, however, you find that they are taking too long to develop, there's a way of speeding up the process. Take some dried-out cowpats and mix them with water until you've produced a substance with a treacle-like consistency. Using an old paintbrush, spread the mixture over the rocks to a thickness of 2–3 mm. Another possible alternative is a porridge mixture made out of milk and oats.

The result will be a thriving colony of fungi, lichens and mosses. It helps if you can maintain an even humidity at a temperature of around 59°F (15°C), so the best time to do this is during damp weather in the summer.

Some typical gardens

Here are two working examples of possible plant combinations for a shaded rock garden. As with the previous examples for sunny situations, the species and varieties we have chosen are generally available at nurseries and garden centres, so you should have no trouble getting hold of any of them.

The plant names are keyed into the pictures as follows: the bold letters and numbers refer to the circled letters (for shrubs) and numbers (for other plants) in the picture; each is followed by the number of plants recommended for the species or variety.

Variety is possible even in the shade

Requirements: a shady, north-westerly aspect, sunlit in summer between 6 and 8 am, but softly shaded by trees during the day and totally shaded by buildings from 7 pm onwards. Total area: 20 ft × 23 ft = 460 sq ft (6 m × 7 m = 42 m^2). Rock materials: limestone and tufa covering an area of 130 sq ft (12 m^2).

The soft shade of trees offers some interesting possibilities for rock gardens, as the variable shade conditions are ideal for some plants. The layout shown here is easy to maintain and can be installed in many existing gardens. It may also be suitable for a front garden, a seating area or an open-air courtyard.

See previous column for an explanation of this key.

A 10 *Arctostaphylos uva-ursi*
B 3 *Buxus sempervirens*
C 1 *Corylopsis pauciflora*
D 5 *Cotoneaster procumbens*
E 1 *Daphne mezereum*
F 5 *Muehlenbeckia axillaris*
G 3 *Rhododendron hirsutum*
H 5 *Vaccinium myrtillus*
I 5 *Vaccinium vitis-idaea*
J 1 *Viburnum carlesii*
K 3 *Microbiota decussata*
L 1 *Tsuga canadensis* 'Nana'
1 3 *Adonis amurensis*
2 10 *Ajuga reptans*
3 5 *Alchemilla alpina*
4 10 *Anemone nemorosa* 'Alba Plena'
5 5 *Anemonopsis macrophylla*
6 10 *Asarum caudatum*
7 5 *Buglossoides purpurocaerulea*
8 10 *Cardamine trifolia*
9 10 *Chiastophyllum oppositifolium*
10 3 *Cypripedium calceolus*
11 10 *Hacquetia epipactis*
12 5 *Hepatica nobilis*
13 5 *Hepatica transsilvanica*
14 10 *Maianthemum bifolium*
15 15 *Omphalodes verna*
16 5 *Polygonatum verticillatum*
17 3 *Ramonda myconi*
18 10 *Sanguinaria canadensis* 'Plena'
19 20 *Saxifraga hypnoides* var. *egemmulosa*
20 10 *Saxifraga cuneifolia*
21 5 *Saxifraga rotundifolia*
22 10 *Soldanella montana*
23 10 *Vancouveria hexandra*
24 5 *Waldsteinia ternata*
25 3 *Asplenium adiantum-nigrum*
26 3 *Asplenium scolopendrium*
27 3 *Polystichum lonchitis*
28 5 *Polypodium vulgare*
29 3 *Deschampsia caespitosa*
30 3 *Melica uniflora*

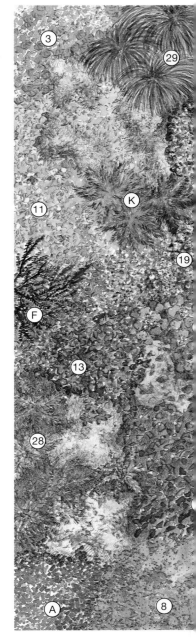

The rocks used are all various forms of limestone. Their light surface colouring creates a cheerier atmosphere in the more shaded parts of the garden, and makes the layout altogether more friendly. If the site slopes at all, it should slope only very gently. You can build the limestone slabs into a dry-stone wall, or simply use them as stepping stones.

Evergreen shrubs such as box (*Buxus*), *Cotoneaster procumbens*, *Rhododendron hirsutum*, bilberry (*Vaccinium myrtillus*) and cowberry (*V. vitis-idaea*) liven up the garden on the dullest of winter days. The conifers provide some structure, and look particularly attractive when they are covered with frost or snow.

The start of the flowering season seems almost unreal as the yellow blooms of *Adonis amurensis* emerge in late February, sometimes pushing up through a layer of snow. Spring proper arrives with the pink, honey-scented blooms of the mezereon (*Daphne mezereum*).

In May and June the garden is dominated by the fragrant white snowball flowers of *Viburnum carlesii*. Its bright-green foliage goes well with the white blooms of the wood anemone (*Anemone nemorosa*), which appear from March onwards, lighting up the gaps between the rocks. The blue tints of the Transylvanian liverleaf (*Hepatica transsilvanica*) compete with those of its native relative (*H. nobilis*), which appear a fortnight later.

Blue-eyed Mary (*Omphalodes verna*) naturally has blue flowers too; these now appear, together with those of the wild ginger (*Asarum*). Towards the end of April the bugle (*Ajuga reptans*) produces yet more blue flowers above its dense mats of leaves.

The yellow *Hacquetia epipactis* emerges into the light from the narrow rock crevices. The pretty, nodding heads of the mountain tassel (*Soldanella montana*) prefer the damper spots. The white blooms of the May lily (*Maianthemum bifolium*) contrast with the larger white flowers of the bloodroot (*Sanguinaria*). Towards the end of May we see the exotic yellow flowers of the lady's slipper (*Cypripedium calceolus*), our largest native orchid, attractively framed by various saxifrages (*Saxifraga*). Amid the rock crevices the flowers of *Ramonda myconi* look quite similar to those of the African violet. Some of the drier spots are home to the trailing stems and pretty flowers of blue gromwell (*Buglossoides purpurocaerulea*), while occasional flowers appear above the green carpet of *Vancouveria hexandra*.

The white, nodding flowers of Solomon's seal (*Polygonatum*) appear from May onwards. This plant grows up to 3 ft (1 m) in height, adopting a dominant position in the garden. In high summer the fleshy-leaved *Chiastophyllum oppositifolium* becomes covered with sprays of golden flowers, taking centre stage together with the waxy,

columbine-like blooms of the false anemone (*Anemonopsis macrophylla*).

Waldsteinia and bittercress (*Cardamine*) creep along the rock crevices and around evergreen ferns such as the hart's tongue (*Asplenium scolopendrium*) and *Polystichum lonchitis*. Spleenwort (*Asplenium*) and polypody (*Polypodium*) will

colonise the tiniest of cracks in walls or rocks. Tussock grass (*Deschampsia*) and melic grass (*Melica*) add to the atmosphere of the garden in autumn, while the leaves of the bearberry (*Arctostaphylos uva-ursi*) turn a gorgeous copper colour.

In November you should take care to remove all the fallen leaves that have blown onto the garden, but there's no need to remove old seedheads until the following March; they can look quite attractive in winter. The variable shade encourages the growth of mosses and lichens, but you can help them still more by watering the rocks as well as the flowers when the weather is dry during the summer period.

 Look at the vegetation that grows in the shade in wild, rocky places such as thick mountain forests or the shaded areas below cliffs and gorges. You'll be amazed at the variety of plants that will grow there — living proof that a rock garden can succeed even in the shade.

A rock garden in a small space

Requirements: a shady, northerly aspect, well lit (but never sunlit) on early summer mornings, and totally shaded by buildings from late morning onwards. Total garden area: 13 ft × 13 ft = 169 sq ft (4 m × 4 m = 16 m²). Rock materials: red sandstone covering an area of 43 sq ft (4 m²).

Your garden may be small and permanently shaded by buildings, wall or fences, but this doesn't mean you can't have a rock garden.

The layout described overleaf has been created around some pieces of red sandstone; it's a marvellous way of turning a small forecourt, back yard or central courtyard into a pleasant little garden.

This rock garden with its babbling brook provides both rest and refreshment.

This garden is ideal for collectors of rare plants. The red sandstone works just as well on a sloping site as on a level one, and looks really good when it is surrounded by perennials, with dark-coloured conifers in the background.

If you put some extra humus in the soil, you'll be able to add woodland shrubs to your collection. Dwarf birch (*Betula nana*) creeps over the rocks, while partridge berry (*Gaultheria procumbens*), cowberry (*Vaccinium vitis-idaea*) and bog bilberry (*V. uliginosum*) stay equally close to the ground. *Daphne burkwoodii* 'Somerset' seems almost to tower above these plants, producing fragrant white blossoms in May and June. Dwarf spruces (*Picea abies*) and creeping yew (*Taxus baccata*) create a pleasant framework for this miniature landscape. They grow only very slowly, and it will be many years before they need pruning to retain their shape.

The perennials have been carefully chosen to provide flowers all year round. Both the Christmas rose (*Helleborus niger*) and the winter-flowering cyclamen (*Cyclamen coum*) flower from late autumn right through to the early spring. The cyclamen varies in colour from white through pink to red, while the Christmas rose makes an excellent cut flower, lasting several weeks in a vase. The first white blooms of the rock cress (*Arabis*) appear in mid-March above a dense mat of deep-green leaves that look really strange among the rock crevices. The pretty, yellow flowers of the twin-flowered violet (*Viola biflora*) appear in the shade of the shrubs.

The barrenwort (*Epimedium*) arrives with the first leaves in March. At the same time the Siberian bugloss (*Brunnera macrophylla*) produces a sea of bright blue out of a dense clump of leaves. The nearby *Jeffersonia diphylla* bears fragile, solitary white flowers on individual stalks. The Japanese poppy (*Hylomecon japonicum*) puts out its soft-green shoots to greet the flowers of the alpine columbine (*Aquilegia alpina*).

In early May the flat, green mats of mossy saxifrage (*Saxifraga × arendsii*) are covered with white, pink or red flowers, while the Dutchman's breeches (*Dicentra cucullaria*) produces strange flowers like inflated white trousers from among its parsley-like leaves.

The native lady's slipper orchid (*Cypripedium calceolus*) reveals the first of its yellow, slipper-like flowers in mid-May. This is closely followed by its North American relative, *Cypripedium parviflorum*, which is smaller in every respect. At the beginning of June we see the large pink-and-white blooms of the showy lady's slipper orchid (*Cypripedium reginae*) — probably the most impressive of all the perennials you can grow in a shaded rock garden. *Dactylorhiza maculata* comes into bloom at the same time — an orchid valued as much for its spotted leaves as for its lovely pink-and-white flowers. To grow these orchids you must ensure that the conditions for them are exactly the same as they would be in the wild. Inorganic fertiliser is the kiss of death for such plants.

Mid-July is time for the yellow or pink flowers of various *Primula* species. They are soon dwarfed by the white martagon lily (*Lilium martagon* 'Album'), with its flowers gushing like

fountains from the green under-growth. The beautifully fragrant pink flowers of *Cyclamen purpurascens* spring up close to the ground, followed in August by the white, pink and red blooms of the ivy-leaved cyclamen (*C. hederifolium*). The last of its flowers coincide with the first of its white-patterned leaves, which remain on the plant throughout the winter.

Yet more flowers follow with the approach of the autumn. *Kirengeshoma palmata* pro-duces gorgeous, waxy yellow flowers above tall, thick clumps of leaves. From September onwards the moisture-loving Japanese toadlily (*Tricyrtis hirta*) produces a series of exotic blooms, most of them white or violet-coloured with a sprinkling of darker spots. Finally, *Saxifraga fortunei* rounds off the main flowering season, its white flowers appearing in profusion above the red leaves with their red, lacquer-coloured stalks. This lovely saxifrage species devel-ops thick mats of leaves as it gets older.

The eventual return of the Christmas rose (*Helleborus niger*) in January heralds the beginning of the next year, and the repeat of the annual cycle.

See page 66 for an explanation of this key.

A 3 *Betula nana*
B 1 *Daphne burkwoodii* 'Somerset'
C 5 *Gaultheria procumbens*
D 5 *Vaccinium uliginosum*
E 3 *Vaccinium vitis-idaea*
F 1 *Picea abies* 'Echiniformis'
G 1 *Picea abies* 'Little Gem'
H 1 *Taxus baccata* 'Repandens'
1 5 *Aquilegia alpina*
2 3 *Aquilegia caerulea*
3 10 *Arabis procurrens*
4 3 *Asarina procumbens*
5 5 *Azorella trifurcata*
6 3 *Brunnera macrophylla*
7 5 *Cyclamen coum*
8 3 *Cyclamen hederifolium*
9 3 *Cyclamen purpurascens*
10 1 *Cypripedium calceolus*
11 1 *Cypripedium reginae*
12 1 *Cypripedium parviflorum*
13 3 *Dactylorhiza maculata*
14 3 *Dicentra cucullaria*
15 5 *Epimedium grandiflorum*
16 1 *Helleborus niger*
17 3 *Hylomecon japonicum*
18 3 *Jeffersonia diphylla*
19 1 *Kirengeshoma palmata*
20 5 *Lilium martagon* 'Album'
21 3 *Primula bulleyana*
22 5 *Primula florindae*
23 5 *Saxifraga* × *arendsii*
24 3 *Tricyrtis hirta*
25 3 *Viola biflora*
26 5 *Asplenium ruta-muraria*
27 3 *Asplenium trichomanes*
28 3 *Asplenium viride*
29 3 *Blechnum spicant*
30 3 *Carex plantaginea*

A selection of rock-garden plants for a shaded site

Perennials

Adonis amurensis
Flowers: Feb.–Apr., various yellow tints.
Growth height: 6–12 in (15–30 cm).
Soil: humus-rich.
Propagation: division.
Comments: this is a gorgeous early-flowering perennial that will even flower in the snow. Its finely divided foliage appears at the end of March.

Left Adonis amurensis *can flower as early as February, even with snow on the ground.*

Right *The wood anemone (*Anemone nemorosa*) is a widespread native perennial.*

The plant dies back at the beginning of June, but you can grow various companion plants such as liverleaf (*Hepatica*) or May lily (*Maianthemum*) in order to fill the gaps.

Bugle
Ajuga reptans
Flowers: Apr.–Jun., blue, occasionally white or pink.
Growth height: 3–6 in (8–15 cm).
Soil: humus-rich.
Propagation: division or rosette cuttings.
Comments: colourful leaf rosettes make this plant attractive even outside the flowering season. Remove excess plant growth to stop it from proliferating. Bugle looks really good

next to water, or in front of an old tree stump.

Wood anemone
Anemone nemorosa
Flowers: Mar.–May, white, blue, purple; occasional greenish and double forms.
Growth height: 4–5 in (10–12 cm).
Soil: loosely structured.
Propagation: rhizome division or seed.
Comments: the wood anemone is a vigorous wild perennial with an unstoppable tendency to spread, but it doesn't overdominate the garden. Its pretty flowers and finely divided leaves die back in May, so you should plant it between mat-forming deciduous perennials that can spread to fill the gaps.

Purple columbine
Aquilegia atrata
Flowers: Apr.–May, black to dark blue.
Growth height: 10–18 in (25–45 cm).
Soil: humus-rich.
Propagation: seed.
Comments: a vigorous wild perennial that forms loose clumps of fine, leathery shoots. Purple columbine is suitable for landscape-type gardens. It has conspicuously coloured flowers, and self-seeds profusely, so it's best to remove seedheads. The foliage is liable to fungal attack; if you do come across such an attack, be careful to remove all affected parts of the plant.

Rock cress
Arabis ferdinandi-coburgii
Flowers: Apr.–Jun., white.
Growth height: 3–6 in
(8–15 cm).
Soil: humus-rich.
Propagation: cuttings or
division.
Comments: an undemanding
ground-cover plant that forms
thick carpets of green leaves;
good for planting under overhanging conifers.

Asarabacca
Asarum europaeum
Flowers: Apr.–May, reddish
brown, insignificant.
Growth height: 4–5 in (10–12
cm).
Soil: loosely structured with
plenty of humus.
Propagation: division.
Comments: forms attractive
ground cover around shrubs
and between the rocks; the
leaves are shiny green and
kidney-shaped, often hiding the
flowers; looks good next to
clematis or anemones; young
plants take 15 months to come
to full maturity.

Siberian bugloss
Brunnera macrophylla
Flowers: Apr.–May, blue.
Growth height: 12–16 in
(30–40 cm).
Soil: humus-rich.
Propagation: seed or division.
Comments: one of the most
conspicuous of all the early-

*Siberian bugloss (*Brunnera macrophylla*) is one of the most important
spring-flowering perennials.*

flowering perennials, with blue
flowers that are yellow inside.
It can be planted either alone
or in small groups. Siberian
bugloss goes well with the
yellow flowers of *Waldsteinia*
or the white sprays of the foam
flower (*Tiarella*). The foliage

appears soon after the flowers
have wilted, and also needs
plenty of room.

Chiastophyllum oppositifolium
Flowers: Jun.–Jul., yellow.
Growth height: 5–6 in
(12–15 cm).
Soil: humus-rich.
Propagation: seed or division.
Comments: this plant looks
highly individual in shaded
locations; it is reminiscent of
wallpepper, with attractive
sprays of flowers, and looks
good with wood sorrel (*Oxalis*)
or liverleaf (*Hepatica*). It forms
thick clumps of fleshy leaves.

Kenilworth ivy
Cymbalaria muralis
Flowers: Apr.–Oct., blue and
white, occasionally pure white

Left *Purple columbine (*Aquilegia
atrata*), noted for its striking flowers,
is a protected species in the wild.*

Growth height: 2-3 in (5-8 cm).
Soil: loosely structured.
Propagation: seed or cuttings.
Comments: this is a vigorous ground-cover plant with leafy shoots growing to 3 ft (1 m) in length. It thrives in the shade of walls. Kenilworth ivy is long-flowering, with masses of tiny flowers; it does rather have a tendency to proliferate, but can be held in check by removing the longer shoots.

Lady's slipper orchid
Cypripedium calceolus
Flowers: May–Jun., yellow and brown.
Growth height: 10-16 in (25-40 cm).
Soil: humus-rich soil on a limestone base.
Propagation: only by careful division of older clumps; seed propagation is possible only under strictly sterile laboratory conditions.

Left *Kenilworth ivy (Cymbalaria muralis) takes root in all the cracks in the rocks.*

Right *The lady's slipper orchid (Cypripedium calceolus) is one of our rarest native orchids.*

Comments: a rare native woodland orchid, strictly protected in the wild, and probably one of the rarest of all plants suitable for shaded rock gardens. The lady's slipper orchid forms loose clumps of stems, each bearing 3-5 leaves and a terminal bloom. It looks really good planted next to liverleaf (*Hepatica*), wood sorrel (*Oxalis*) or small ferns.

Showy lady's slipper orchid
Cypripedium reginae
Flowers: Jun., red, pink and white.
Growth height: 14-26 in (35-65 cm).

Soil: humus-rich.
Propagation/comments: see lady's slipper orchid.

Dactylorhiza maculata
Flowers: Jun.–Jul., pink with white.
Growth height: 14-26 in (35-60 cm).
Soil: humus-rich.
Propagation: only possible by seed under sterile laboratory conditions; rarely self-seeds spontaneously.
Comments: here is yet another valuable orchid; its underground tuber puts out a stem bearing 3-6 leaves and a single flower. For other points see lady's slipper orchid.

Barrenwort
Epimedium alpinum
Flowers: Apr.–May, yellow.
Growth height: 10-14 in (25-35 cm).
Soil: humus-rich.
Propagation: division.
Comments: barrenwort is a beautiful wild perennial with shiny green foliage. You can put it in front of shrubs or tree stumps, and it looks particularly good next to small ferns or blue-eyed Mary (*Omphalodes verna*). The foliage turns copper-coloured in autumn, and may stay on the plant all through the winter.

Christmas rose
Helleborus niger
Flowers: Jan.–Mar., whitish to pink.
Growth height: 10-14 in (25-35 cm).

Soil: humus-rich soil, preferably on a limestone base.
Propagation: seed or division.
Comments: this is a favourite garden perennial. It is clump-forming, with pretty flowers and strong, shiny green leaves that stay on the plant all winter. The Christmas rose looks particularly attractive in front of dwarf conifers and/or next to clematis or liverleaf (*Hepatica*).

Liverleaf
Hepatica nobilis
Flowers: Mar.–Apr., blue, occasionally pink or white.
Growth height: 4–6 in (10–15 cm).
Soil: humus-rich soil on a limestone base.
Propagation: by division or by seed from older clumps.
Comments: this is an early-flowering wild perennial with decorative foliage that goes marvellously with most other shade-loving perennials. The leaves form loose clumps, and appear only after the flowers

have gone; liverleaf will often self-seed under favourable conditions.

Kirengeshoma palmata
Flowers: Aug.–Oct., yellow.
Growth height: 2–4 ft (60–120 cm).
Soil: humus-rich.
Propagation: by division or by seed from older clumps.
Comments: *Kirengeshoma palmata* is a tall, very stately plant that looks particularly impressive when in flower; its upright stems bear drooping clusters of flowers.

May lily
Maianthemum bifolium
Flowers: May–Jun., white.
Growth height: 2–3 in (6–8 cm).
Soil: humus-rich.
Propagation: division.
Comments: this is an attractive wild perennial with soft foliage and flowers resembling lily-of-the-valley. It goes well with many other woodland plants,

and spreads out vigorously if planted with wood sorrel (*Oxalis*), forming extensive mats of leaves.

Blue-eyed Mary
Omphalodes verna
Flowers: Apr.–Jun., blue, occasionally white.
Growth height: 5–6 in (12–15 cm).
Soil: loosely structured, humus-rich soil.
Propagation: division.
Comments: blue-eyed Mary is one of the commonest wild perennials for shaded gardens — an attractive plant that makes a good transition to other parts of garden, and looks good next to foam flower (*Tiarella*). The foliage appears after flowering has begun.

Left *The Christmas rose (*Helleborus niger*) grows well when lightly shaded by shrubs.*

Right *The May lily (*Maianthemum bifolium*) forms dense mats of leaves on humus-rich soil.*

Solomon's seal
Polygonatum × hybridum
Flowers: May, white.
Growth height: 14–39 in
(35–100 cm).
Soil: loosely structured, humus-rich soil.
Propagation: seed or division.
Comments: Solomon's seal is a native wild perennial with a tall, elegant growth habit and pendant flowers. It goes very well with small ferns and loosely growing ground-cover plants, and produces blue seedheads in late summer which look very attractive. Moreover, the shoots turn a particularly lovely yellow colour in autumn.

Blue cowslip, lungwort
Pulmonaria angustifolia
Flowers: Mar.–Apr., blue, occasional white and red tints.
Growth height: 10–12 in
(25–30 cm).
Soil: humus-rich.
Propagation: division.
Comments: the blue cowslip is a smallish-leaved, early-flowering wild perennial with beautiful flowers that appear at much the same time as the foliage. If mildew occurs, you should cut out all the affected parts completely.

Sagina subulata 'Aurea'
Flowers: Apr.–Jul., white.
Growth height: 1–1½ in
(2–4 cm).
Soil: loosely structured, humus-rich soil.
Propagation: cuttings or division.

Blue-eyed Mary (Omphalodes verna) comes from the mountains of south-east Europe.

Solomon's seal is a perennial that thrives in partial shade.

Comments: an interesting, moss-like perennial with yellow-coloured shoots that spread to form a continuous carpet; *Sagina subulata* 'Aurea' is particularly effective planted in the narrow cracks between paving or stepping stones.

Mossy saxifrage
Saxifraga × arendsii
Flowers: Apr.–Jun., white, pink and red tints, occasionally yellowish.
Growth height: 3–6 in
(8–15 cm).
Soil: gravelly.
Propagation: seed, cuttings or division.
Comments: mossy saxifrage is an attractive ground-cover plant with mats of fleshy leaf rosettes. Unfortunately blackbirds seem to regard it as a particularly choice morsel, so you may need to protect it with black threads. This is a good choice for an edging plant.

Saxifraga umbrosa
Flowers: May–Jun., white with red spots.
Growth height: 3–5 in
(8–12 cm).
Soil: humus-rich.
Propagation: cuttings or division.
Comments: *Saxifraga umbrosa* is a vigorous and undemanding ground-cover plant that is often employed as an edging for flower beds or for groups of plants. It will form dense mats of leaf rosettes, with strong, oval-shaped leaves.

76

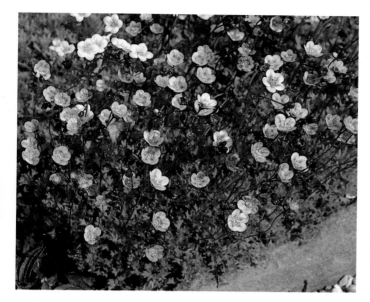

Vancouveria hexandra
Flowers: May–Jun., white.
Growth height: 8-12 in (20-30 cm).
Soil: humus-rich.
Propagation: division.
Comments: *Vancouveria hexandra* is an attractive perennial for planting beneath small shrubs, and it also thrives in rock crevices. The compound leaves are made up of kidney-shaped leaflets, and the strange-looking flowers are borne in loose sprays. You should treat this plant with great respect as it tends to be invasive.

Waldsteinia geoides
Flowers: Apr.–May, yellow.
Growth height: 6-8 in (15-20 cm).
Soil: humus-rich.
Propagation: cuttings or division.
Comments: the leaves and flowers of *Waldsteinia geoides* are highly reminiscent of wild strawberry. It copes well with crowded perennial beds, and can also be good for ground cover or for planting in dry spots. This plant is tolerant of shrub roots, but you should remove longer shoots to stop the plant proliferating.

Mountain tassel
Soldanella montana
Flowers: Apr.-Jun., blue, occasionally white.
Growth height: 1-3 in (3-8 cm).
Soil: humus-rich.
Propagation: seed or division.
Comments: together with ferns and liverleaf, the mountain tassel is one of the best companion plants for putting with winter-hardy orchids in special places in the garden. This plant has thin stems that bear round leaves and pendant flowers with quite noticeable fringes.

Japanese toadlily
Tricyrtis hirta
Flowers: Sep.-Nov., pink, red to violet.
Growth height: 10-24 in (25-60 cm).
Soil: humus-rich.
Propagation: seed.

Comments: the Japanese toadlily is a popular woodland garden plant, with exotic and rather unusually shaped flowers. However, the young plants are vulnerable to frost, so you should protect them with brushwood during the first winter after planting.

Ferns

Northern maidenhair fern
Adiantum pedatum
Growth height: 14-20 in (35-50 cm).
Soil: humus-rich.
Propagation: by spores or division.
Comments: an attractive solitary fern that forms dense clumps of largish fronds with shiny green stems and finely divided leaflets. Watch out for the young shoots, which are vulnerable to late frosts. This fern likes narrow rock crevices, and goes well with orchids, wood sorrel (*Oxalis*) or foam flower (*Tiarella*).

Wall spleenwort
Asplenium ruta-muraria
Growth height: 2-3 in (5-8 cm).
Soil: pockets of humus in between stones.
Propagation: by spores or by dividing older clumps.
Comments: an attractive dwarf fern for narrow crevices in dry-stone walls; produces thick clumps of finely divided fronds growing close to the rock or soil surface; looks very good with mosses, saxifrages and Kenilworth ivy (*Cymbalaria muralis*).

Hart's tongue fern
Asplenium scolopendrium
Growth height: 10-20 in (25-50 cm).
Soil: loosely structured.
Propagation: by spores or division.

Comments: forms dense clumps of slender evergreen fronds with rows of brown spores beneath; popular garden fern that comes in many shapes and sizes; looks good next to orchids, wood sorrel (*Oxalis*) or foam flower (*Tiarella*).

Hard fern
Blechnum spicant
Growth height: 4-8 in (10-20 cm).
Soil: loosely structured with plenty of humus.
Propagation: by spores.
Comments: forms large, flat rosettes of dark-green ribbed fronds with black stems; spore capsules appear in summer at base of rosette, releasing brown spores; ideal fern for planting under foliage shrubs together with taller perennials such as *Kirengeshoma palmata* or Solomon's seal (*Polygonatum*).

The fronds of the hart's tongue fern (Asplenium scolopendrium) *remain beautiful even in winter.*

Left Maidenhair ferns (Adiantum) *are among the most valuable of garden ferns.*

Right The hard fern (Blechnum spicant) *forms thick clumps with the passage of time.*

Royal fern
Osmunda regalis
Growth height: 16-59 in
(40-150 cm).
Soil: humus-rich.
Propagation: by spores.
Comments: the royal fern has a
woody stem, and bears soft,
finely divided fronds with reddish colouring that later turns
green. This is a large but rare
native fern that is strictly protected in the wild. It needs
moist soil, so is best planted
near water.

Common polypody
Polypodium vulgare
Growth height: 4-20 in
(10-50 cm).
Soil: pockets of humus in
cracks in stones or in the bark
of old trees.
Propagation: by spores or
division.
Comments: common polypody
possesses strongly ribbed
evergreen fronds that develop
from creeping rhizomes spreading close to the ground; the
fronds bear scale-like spore
capsules on their undersides.

SHADED ROCK GARDENS

Bulb and tuber plants for rock gardens

Common name / Scientific name	Flower colour / Flowering period	Other comments
Anemone blanda	light blue / March–April	varieties: 'Radar', 'White Splendour'
Italian cuckoo pint / *Arum italicum*	whitish yellow / April–May	plant in groups
spring meadow saffron / *Bulbocodium vernum*	purplish red / March–April	clump-forming
glory-of-the-snow / *Chionodoxa luciliae*	blue / March–April	plant in groups
autumn crocus / *Colchicum* hybrids	white, lilac, pink / October–November	varieties: 'Waterlily', 'The Giant'
Crocus speciosus	blue / September–October	clump-forming
Crocus tommasinianus	blue / February–March	plant in large groups
winter-flowering cyclamen / *Cyclamen coum*	red, pink / December–April	plant in groups
winter aconite / *Erianthis hyemalis*	yellow / January–February	plant in groups
dog's tooth violet / *Erythronium dens-canis*	pink / March–April	clump-forming
crown imperial / *Fritillaria imperialis*	red / April–May	clump-forming
common snowdrop / *Galanthus nivalis*	white / February–March	plant in groups
Iris danfordiae	yellow / February–March	clump-forming
Iris reticulata	dark blue / February–March	clump-forming
spring snowflake / *Leucojum vernum*	white / March–April	clump-forming
martagon lily / *Lilium martagon*	red–white / June–July	clump-forming
dwarf lily / *Lilium pumilum*	red / June–August	clump-forming
grape hyacinth / *Muscari armeniacum*	blue / April–May	forms spikes
Greig's tulip / *Tulipa greigii*	scarlet with yellow / April–May	
Tulipa praestans	scarlet / April–May	several flowers on each stem

Broad-leaved shrubs

Abeliophyllum distichum
Flowers: Feb.–Apr., whitish pink.
Growth habit: 7½ ft (2.25 m) high by 5 ft (1.5 m) wide.
Soil: humus-rich.
Comments: an attractive, very early-flowering shrub for planting around edges or in front of conifers; it has beautiful autumn colouring.

Japanese maple
Acer japonicum 'Aconitifolium'
Flowers: Apr.–May, yellowish green.
Growth habit: 13 ft (4 m) high by 5 ft (1.5 m) wide.
Soil: humus-rich.
Comments: the foliage of the Japanese maple is reminiscent of wolfsbane (*Aconitum*), with coppery or red tints in spring and autumn, and a slightly drooping habit. Japanese maple makes an excellent edge plant, and is particularly attractive near water.

Bearberry
Arctostaphylos uva-ursi
Flowers: Apr.–Jun., pinkish white.
Growth habit: up to 5 ft (150 cm) high by 31 in (80 cm) wide.
Soil: humus in rock pockets.
Comments: bearberry is an evergreen dwarf shrub with leathery leaves, and spreads by means of long shoots to form dense ground cover. This is a particularly good shrub for planting on rocks or beneath dense conifers.

Dwarf birch
Betula nana
Flowers: Apr.–May, yellowish, insignificant.
Growth habit: up to 2 ft (60 cm) high by 5 ft (150 cm) wide.
Soil: humus-rich.

Comments: *Betula nana* is a creeping dwarf tree with dark-brown stems and small, shiny leaves. It's an excellent dwarf species for planting in front of large rocks, or as a link to a heather garden.

Caryopteris × *clandonensis*
Flowers: Jul.–Aug., blue to violet tints.
Growth habit: up to 47 in (1.2 m) high by 39 in (1 m) wide.
Soil: gravelly.
Comments: this plant looks attractive even outside the flowering season, with greyish leaves borne on thin shoots. *Caryopteris* × *clandonensis* looks beautiful in a large, sunny garden, and goes well with catmint (*Nepeta*) or rock cress (*Arabis*). Prune it in April to encourage new growth.

Alpina clematis
Clematis alpina
Flowers: Apr.–May, blue and white.
Growth habit: up to 13 ft (4 m) high by 7 ft (2 m) wide.
Soil: loosely structured, humus-rich soil.
Comments: the long, thin leafy shoots climb over rocks and other shrubs, spreading all over the garden. Prune the Alpina clematis in June to encourage denser growth.

Alpina clematis (Clematis alpina) produces a gorgeous display of flowers in May.

Left *The flowers of the buttercup winter hazel (Corylopsis pauciflora) often appear at the beginning of March.*

Right *The mezereon (Daphne mezereum) is one of the most important early-flowering plants to be found in a rock garden.*

Buttercup winter hazel
Corylopsis pauciflora
Flowers: Mar.–May, yellowish.
Growth habit: up to 13 ft (4 m) high by 8 ft (2.5 m) wide.
Soil: loosely structured, humus-rich soil.
Comments: an early-flowering shrub with small, drooping flowers and hazel-like foliage; the buttercup winter hazel makes a suitable link plant between a rock garden and a heather garden, and goes well with larger conifers.

Mezereon
Daphne mezereum
Flowers: Mar.–May, red and pink, occasionally white.
Growth habit: up to 6 ft (1.8 m) high by 5 ft (1.5 m) wide.
Soil: humus-rich.
Comments: this native woodland shrub produces fragrant flowers in early spring; an excellent link plant between rock garden and perennial beds.
Danger: the red fruits are very poisonous, and should always be removed and destroyed while still green, especially if there's any risk of children taking them.

Garland flower
Daphne cneorum
Flowers: Apr.–Jun., red, pink, occasionally white.
Growth habit: 12 in (30 cm) high by 20 in (50 cm) wide.

Soil: humus-rich.
Comments: the dark shoots of the garland flower grow down to rest on the ground, and bear narrow green leaves that make the plant attractive even when it's not in flower; this shrub grows very well in narrow cracks, and can also look very good in groups.

Fothergilla major
Flowers: Apr.–May, white.
Growth habit: up to 8 ft (2.5 m) high by 5 ft (1.5 m) wide.
Soil: humus-rich.
Comments: especially attractive in flowering season, when it's covered with fluffy white blooms; *Fothergilla major* has gorgeous red or copper autumn colouring. It likes an open, solitary position, and looks good in front of walls, dark rocks or groups of conifers.

Left *Witch hazels (*Hamamelis*) are among the finest of all the winter-flowering shrubs.*

Right *In this country, rhododendrons (*Rhododendron *species and varieties) have become well established in the wild.*

Broom
Genista lydia
Flowers: May–Jun., yellow.
Growth habit: up to 16 in (40 cm) high by 24 in (60 cm) wide.
Soil: gravelly.
Comments: this beautiful garden shrub will creep along the tops of walls to form a dense mass of intertwining branches, and in the late spring it is simply covered with bright-yellow flowers. *Genista lydia* can look really good in the company of perennials such as catmint (*Nepeta*) or rock cress (*Arabis*).

Japanese witch hazel
Hamamelis japonica
Flowers: Jan.–Apr., yellow.
Growth habit: up to 8 ft (2.5 m) high by 10 ft (3 m) wide.
Soil: loosely structured.
Comments: Japanese witch hazel is undoubtedly one of the most attractive winter-flowering shrubs. Its pretty yellow flowers appear on leafless branches, and its hazel-like foliage follows in spring. It makes a good background plant.

Winter jasmine
Jasminum nudiflorum
Flowers: Nov.–Mar., yellow.
Growth habit: up to 2 ft (60 cm) high by 5 ft (150 cm) wide.
Soil: loosely structured.
Comments: winter jasmine creeps over stones, hangs from walls or climbs up rocks or trees by means of its long, thin shoots. It's an attractive winter-flowering shrub, and ideal for conspicuous positions: you could, for instance, position it on a wall or in front of a rock. Prune it back drastically in summer so as to encourage new growth.

Dwarf Russian almond
Prunus tenella
Flowers: Apr.–May, red and pink, occasionally white.
Growth habit: up to 20 in (50 cm) high by 40 in (1 m) wide.
Soil: gravelly.
Comments: the dwarf Russian almond is an attractive flowering shrub that produces dark-coloured branches with dark-green foliage from underground shoots. The flower buds appear in early spring on older wood, followed by attractive blossom. *Prunus tenella* is an excellent shrub for planting in rock crevices together with aubrietia (*Aubrieta*) or soapwort (*Saponaria*).

Rhododendron ferrugineum
Flowers: Apr.–Jun., pink and red.
Growth habit: up to 24 in (60 cm) high by 40 in (1 m) wide.
Soil: pockets of humus in limestone.

The catkins of this dwarf willow (Salix hastata 'Wehrhahnii') are a feast for the eyes.

Comments: an attractive evergreen rhododendron from the mountains of continental Europe, this dwarf shrub goes well with large ferns in the shade of trees.

Rhododendron hirsutum
Flowers: May–Jul., pink and red.
Growth habit: up to 31 in (80 cm) high by 4 ft (120 cm) wide.
Soil: acid, humus-rich.
Comments: this is a European evergreen rhododendron with purplish-pink flowers.

Dwarf willow
Salix hastata 'Wehrhahnii'
Flowers: Apr.–May, yellow stamens and conspicuous white catkins.
Growth habit: up to 4 ft (1.2 m) high by 5 ft (1.5 m) wide.
Soil: loosely structured.
Comments: this interesting dwarf willow variety has thin, light-brown shoots borne on loose branches and covered with pretty catkins in spring. It makes an excellent link plant between rock gardens and heather gardens.

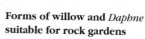

Forms of willow and *Daphne* suitable for rock gardens

Garland flower (*Daphne cneorum*):
D. c. 'Eximia', 10 in (25 cm), pink
D. c. var. *pygmaea*, 2 in (5 cm), pink
D. c. var. *pygmaea* 'Alba', 2 in (5 cm), white
D. juliae, 14 in (35 cm), pink, red
D. oleoides, 12 in (30 cm), light carmine
D. petrea, 4 in (10 cm), carmine
D. sericea, 14 in (35 cm), salmon pink

Willow (*Salix*):
S. arbuscula, 2 in (5 cm)
S. 'Boydii', 20 in (50 cm)
S. × *grahamii*, 12 in (30 cm)
S. herbecea, 1–2 in (2–5 cm)
S. reticulata, 2 in (5 cm)
S. retusa, 10 in (25 cm)
S. serpillifolia, 3 in (8 cm)
S. × *simulatrix*, 12 in (30 cm)

Coniferous shrubs

Dwarf balsam fir
Abies balsamea 'Nana'
Growth habit: up to 24 in (60 cm) high by 31 in (80 cm) wide.
Soil: loosely structured.
Comments: this is a dwarf conifer with a broad spherical habit and dark-green needles; it looks good in small groups, especially when it is planted near rocks.

Dwarf Lawson cypress
Chamaecyparis lawsoniana 'Minima Glauca'
Growth habit: up to 24 in (60 cm) high by 16 in (40 cm) wide.

Soil: humus-rich.
Comments: the dwarf Lawson cypress is a compact shrub with a broad spherical habit and bearing blue-green, scale-like needles. It can be pruned into fascinating shapes, and is shown to its best advantage when planted next to yellow-needled yews or cypresses. It also makes an ideal plant for troughs and other containers.

Dwarf Hinoki cypress
Chamaecyparis obtusa 'Nana Gracilis'
Growth habit: up to 31 in (80 cm) high by 24 in (60 cm) wide.
Soil: humus-rich with a certain amount of loam.
Comments: this is a dwarf conifer with a spherical habit and bearing dark-green, scale-like needles. The bark is noted for its strange, twisted surface pattern. The dwarf Hinoki cypress can be successfully pruned into various bonsai-like forms. However, it really needs to be planted in a solitary situation.

Dwarf Sawara cypress
Chamaecyparis pisifera 'Filifera Aurea Nana'
Growth habit: up to 24 in (60 cm) high by 31 in (80 cm) wide.
Soil: loosely structured.

The dwarf balsam fir (Abies balsamea 'Nana') grows quite beautiful with age.

Comments: this dwarf conifer has a spherical habit, drooping branches and yellow needles; the drooping branches make it a particularly good shrub for placing next to large rocks or tree stumps.

Creeping common juniper
Juniperus communis 'Hornibrookii'
Growth habit: up to 12 in (30 cm) high by 79 in (2 m) wide.
Soil: loosely structured with a high humus content.
Comments: this is an unusual creeping variety of the common juniper (which is normally tall and slim). The sharp needles are bright green with silvery edges. It looks good when creeping over rocks, and can be pruned to shape.

Blue Chinese juniper
Juniperus chinensis 'Blaauw'
Growth habit: up to 6 ft (1.8 m) high by 2 ft (60 cm) wide.
Soil: humus-rich.
Comments: a medium-sized conifer with a narrow conical habit and dense grey-blue needles. This juniper looks good in small groups, and is very tolerant of pruning.

Blue creeping juniper
Juniperus horizontalis 'Glauca'
Growth habit: up to 12 in (30 cm) high by 79 in (2 m) wide.
Soil: loosely structured.
Comments: this is a creeping conifer, densely branching, with steel-blue, scale-like needles; it is valuable and extremely attractive.

Left *The creeping juniper* Juniperus horizontalis *'Glauca' will colonise the tiniest of rock crevices.*

Right *The pygmy spruce (*Picea abies *'Pygmaea') must grow old to achieve this unusual crouching habit.*

Blue flaky juniper
Juniperus squamata 'Blue Star'
Growth habit: up to 12 in (30 cm) high by 39 in (1 m) wide.
Soil: loosely structured.
Comments: a dense, bushy dwarf conifer with sharp, upright, silvery-blue needles; plant in small groups.

Dwarf spruce
Picea abies 'Echiniformis'
Growth habit: up to 20 in (50 cm) high by 39 in (1 m) wide.

Soil: loosely structured.
Comments: this is a dwarf conifer with a spherical habit and grey-green needle. It looks beautiful in narrow rock crevices, and can be trained into bonsai-like shapes.

Blue dwarf spruce
Picea abies 'Pumila Glauca'
Growth habit: up to 31 in (80 cm) high by 24 in (60 cm) wide.
Soil: loosely structured.
Comments: the blue dwarf spruce is a dwarf conifer with a broad spherical habit, dense shoots and bluish-green needles; it looks good as a solitary, and is very tolerant of pruning.

*Dwarf pines (*Pinus *varieties) are an ideal shrub for the rock garden.*

Pygmy spruce
Picea abies 'Pygmaea'
Growth habit: up to 28 in (70 cm) high by 31 in (80 cm) wide.
Soil: loosely structured.
Comments: the pygmy spruce is an attractive dwarf conifer with a broad spherical habit and bearing bright-green, spirally arranged needles. Plant this tree as a solitary in front of large rocks.

Dwarf pine
Pinus mugo pumila
Growth habit: up to 16 in (40 cm) high by 79 in (2 m) wide.
Soil: loosely structured.
Comments: this dwarf conifer possesses a broad, densely branching habit and its needles are deep green in colour. It looks good in small groups, and is tolerant of pruning.

Dwarf Siberian pine
Pinus pumila 'Glauca'
Growth habit: up to 20 in (50 cm) high by 39 in (1 m) wide.
Soil: gravelly.
Comments: a dwarf conifer with a broad habit, upturned spreading branches and silvery-blue needles. Its attractive habit can be further improved by careful pruning.

Yew
Taxus baccata 'Summer-gold'
Growth habit: up to 31 in (80 cm) high by 79 in (2 m) wide.
Soil: loosely structured.
Comments: a small yew with a broad spreading habit, horizontal branches and shiny-yellow needles that turn bronze-coloured in winter; extremely tolerant of pruning, and best planted as a solitary.

This dwarf hemlock (Tsuga canadensis 'Jeddeloh') has a particularly interesting habit.

American arbor-vitae
Thuja occidentalis 'Danica'
Growth habit: up to 20 in (40 cm) high by 20 in (50 cm) wide.
Soil: loosely structured.
Comments: an attractive dwarf conifer with a broad spherical habit and deep-green scale-like needles, the American arbor-vitae looks very good in small groups and is also very tolerant of pruning.

Dwarf hemlock
Tsuga canadensis 'Jeddeloh'
Growth habit: up to 24 in (60 cm) high by 31 in (80 cm) wide.
Soil: humus-rich.
Comments: this small conifer is characterised by a densely branching, cushion-like habit, and bears a thick covering of fresh-green needles that have a tendency to droop. The dwarf hemlock looks very effective in the company of large groups of stones and can easily be trained by pruning.

Other coniferous shrubs
Abies koreana 'Compact'
24 in (60 cm), greyish green
Cedrus deodara 'Pendula'
12 in (30 cm), light blue-green
Chamaecyparis obtusa 'Goldilocks'
40 in (100 cm), golden yellow
Juniperus communis 'Berkshire'
31 in (80 cm), dark green
Larix kaempferi 'Blue Dwarf'
40 in (100 cm), blue-green
Picea glauca 'Sanders Blue'
40 in (100 cm), dark blue
P. sitchensis 'Silberzwerg'
31 in (80 cm), silvery green
Pinus mugo 'Jakobsen'
20 in (50 cm), dark green
P. m. 'Humpy'
16 in (40 cm), dark green
Tsuga canadensis 'Jeddeloh'
16 in (40 cm), rounded habit
T. c. 'Rugg's Washington'
16 in (40 cm), spreading habit

With careful pruning, any yew (Taxus) can be turned into an attractive dwarf plant.

Water in a rock garden

A rock garden next to a pond

A rock garden built around a pond offers a host of interesting possibilities. You can have rocks right up to the pond edge, with nothing more than a layer of grit and some paving stones to divide them from the water itself.

Such a combination must always be in a sunny location. Large deciduous trees, or even conifers that shed their needles, should be kept well away from the site. Too many fallen leaves may be as detrimental to the pond as to the rock garden.

If you want to find a natural model for such a site, the best place to look is next to a reservoir or stream in the mountains. One particularly attractive idea is to have a small stream running through your rock garden into your pond.

One common reason why people build a rock garden in these circumstances is to make creative use of the material that has been excavated to form the pond. If this is what you are doing, you must make sure the material is properly compacted, so that no soil will be washed down into the pond.

It's important to create a firm boundary between the rock garden and the pond edge. The best solution is a layer of grit with a grain size of 0.1–0.3 in (2–8 mm). The grit has the

effect of filtering any run-off water that drains into the pond during periods of rain.

The pond bank also needs to be readily accessible so it can be properly maintained, and so that visitors can enjoy the site. The best solution here, in both practical and aesthetic terms, is a series of stepping stones made from natural stone combined with grit of various sizes. To prevent frost action displacing the stepping stones, you should bed them on a mixture of one part cement to three parts sand. To fill in the gaps between the stones, use grit with a grain size of ½–1½ in (16–32 mm).

Apart from filtering the run-off water, the grit also allows moisture to filter through from the pond to the rock garden. The surrounding soil tends to absorb moisture from the pond via the grit layer. This can deplete the water in the pond by as much 10 per cent, especially during periods of warm, dry weather, but the water loss will be halted as soon as soon as the soil becomes saturated.

If you want to stop this process happening, you can separate the pond water from the rock garden by extending the pond liner. However, most

pond-edge plants or water-loving rock plants grow much better if the moisture level is regulated by this quite natural process of absorption.

The following plants are particularly suitable for the part of a rock garden bordering the edge of a pond: *Astilbe chinensis*, marsh marigold (*Caltha palustris*), lady's smock (*Cardamine pratensis*), snake's head fritillary (*Fritillaria meleagris*), creeping Jenny (*Lysimachia nummularia*), tufted forget-me-not (*Myosotis caespitosa*), grass of Parnassus (*Parnassia palustris*), giant cowslip (*Primula*

A stream like this sets a rock garden off beautifully.

florindae), two other primulas (*P. helodoxa* and *P. rosea*), and finally globe flower (*Trollius europaeus*).

An artificial stream

An artificial watercourse can be made to look quite amazingly natural, just like a mountain stream running through a rocky landscape.

This is the kind of situation where plastic pond liners come into their own. The water can be pumped up from the pond to the top of the stream, and the liner can be hidden beneath a layer of fine grit with a grain size of 0.1–0.3 in (2–8 mm). If you create a suitable gradient, interrupted by a series of steps, the result will be a delightfully babbling brook.

To ensure the liner can't be punctured by sharp stones, you should lay it down over a protective layer of fine sand about 2 in (5 cm) thick.

An artificial pond

It may be that your garden simply isn't near any naturally occurring water such as a pond or a stream, but that's no reason on its own for doing without water features altogether; you can still create your own small, artificial pond.

Small, ready-made ponds are generally available from builders' merchants and garden centres. They are frequently moulded to an irregular shape, and normally have a capacity of 20–33 gallons (90–150 l). You should always choose a site that is never shaded from the sun.

Start by digging a hole about 8 in (20 cm) deeper and 8 in (20 cm) wider than the actual dimensions of the pond. Now add a 2-in (5-cm) thick layer of sand, compacting it to make it firm. Install the pond, using a spirit level to make sure you've got it level. Finally fill in the gaps around the pond with more sand, stamping it down with your feet to make it firm. The water depth can vary between 10 in (25 cm) and 12 in (30 cm). Cover the edges with paving stones or other flat stones.

Now it's time to install container-grown water plants in the pond. The following are suitable for even the smallest artificial pond: water plantain (*Alisma plantago-aquatica*), flowering rush (*Butomus umbellatus*), frogbit (*Hydrocharis morsus-ranae*), mare's tail (*Hippuris vulgaris*), bog bean (*Menyanthes trifoliata*) and common arrowhead (*Sagittaria sagittifolia*).

As a final touch, put an old branch or a piece of tree root in the pond, with one end protruding out over the side. This means that if any animals fall into the pond they have a chance of climbing out again.

A rock garden on the roof

Small areas of flat roofing are particularly suitable for creating a small rock garden — look at the roof on your garage or garden shed, for example, or perhaps even the roofing over your dustbins.

The only basic requirement is that the roof must be strong enough to carry the weight of a rock garden. Apart from the standard snow load of 14 lb/sq ft (70 kg/m²), you should also allow an additional tolerance of 20-50 lb/sq ft (100-250 kg/m²) if you are going to be able to build a reasonably attractive rock garden.

This means that before you can even start, you need to find out exactly what load your roof can safely bear. The original builders or manufacturers of the building or extension should be able to give you the details you need. If they're not available, or you're still in doubt, then call on the services of a structural engineer. Once you're sure the roof will carry the necessary weight, you can start building your rock garden.

The construction stage

The most suitable material for sealing the roof is a 1-1.5-mm-thick layer of polythene or PVC lining. You'll need to raise the edges of the roof garden by around 4-6 in (10-15 cm) using a wooden frame construction. The best timber to use is planed larchwood, which will stand up to all weathers. Clean the whole area with a broom before laying the roof lining. Use metal brackets to attach the lining to the wooden frame, with the help of a strip of wood all the way round the edge. Finally, make sure there are no gaps left between the lining and the actual roof surface.

Now cover the roof lining with a thick layer of fleece, to prevent the plant roots from puncturing the lining. The most suitable material for this purpose is glass-fibre fleece with a weight of around 1-2 oz/sq ft (400-600 g/m²), but you can use strips of felt instead. You'll need to add a drainage layer around 2 in (4-6 cm) thick on top of the fleece to stop the soil above from becoming waterlogged. The most appropriate materials for this drainage layer are pumice gravel or expanded clay granules.

The final layer of topsoil can be laid directly onto the drainage layer, though some roof gardeners like to separate the two with another layer of glass fibre to stop the plant roots invading the drainage layer. The composition of the topsoil will depend on the plants you intend to grow in it, but in general it can be much the same as that used in any rock garden (see page 12). The soil depth should be between

This roof area has been planted out with a varied selection of stonecrops (Sedum species) to create an interesting thematic garden.

2 in (6 cm) and 6 in (15 cm), depending on the plants that you've chosen.

Place lines of stepping stones on top of the soil so you'll have something to walk on. Now, at last, you can install the rocks and stones. The number you

(3 cm) and 2 in (6 cm) in diameter, so the appropriate planting density will vary accordingly from two to five plants per square foot (18–50/m^2).

Always use a blunt wooden dibber for planting out. Never use a trowel: if you made even the tiniest slip, the sharp edge could damage the roof lining.

When you've finished planting out, water the whole area thoroughly; this will tend to reduce the soil depth a little. Finally, cover the exposed soil between the plants, rocks and stepping stones with a ½–1-in (1–3-cm) layer of mulch. Perhaps the best mulching materials for roof gardens are expanded granules of slate or clay.

If the roof has a slight gradient, there's a definite risk that the soil and plants may be washed away during heavy rain for the first few weeks after planting. For the first six to eight weeks it's a good idea to have some plastic sheeting on hand, ready to cover them up if the heavens suddenly open.

The best time for laying out a roof garden is between March and June, or from late August to late November. Never install such a garden in the heat of the summer or during the main period when frost occurs. If you plant out in autumn, then you'll need to cover the whole area with spruce brushwood during the first winter. Don't remove any dried-out plant material or seedheads until the following spring.

can use will depend for the most part on the weight that the roof can carry.

The planting stage

If the roof garden is clearly visible, then the following rock plants will give you the most attractive display: rock jasmine (*Androsace*), rock cress (*Arabis*), bellflowers (*Campanula*), carnations (*Dianthus*), soapwort (*Saponaria*), saxifrages (*Saxifraga*), stonecrops

(*Sedum*), houseleek (*Sempervivum*), campions (*Silene*) and many others. If the roof surface is more difficult to see, then you're better off using just stonecrops (*Sedum*) and grasses such as fescue (*Festuca*) and bluegrass (*Poa*).

Before you start planting out, set out all the plants in their pots ready for planting. Most alpines for roof gardens are sold in small pots that accommodate root balls between 1 in

A miniature rock garden in a trough or old sink

If you don't have a garden of your own, then the best substitute for a rock garden is a miniature alpine garden in a trough or perhaps some other suitable container.

The ideal receptacle for a collection of alpine shrubs and perennials is an old animal trough or sink made of natural stone. Such containers are both natural-looking and very attractive in themselves. In recent years, however, the antique value of these old stone troughs means they have become rare and sought-after items, fetching astronomical prices in the antique shops.

Fortunately, there are other suitable materials available. A trough or sink made of reconstituted stone or frost-resistant terracotta can also look very effective. Failing that, you could even create a suitable container of your own (see page 94).

There are many possible locations for an alpine collection: a patio or window-sill, for instance, or by the front door — indeed any flat surface where the plants will be properly visible. Sometimes a roof garden may provide the space you require, or a window-sill may be large enough to accommodate a series of bowls or other suitable containers.

Wherever you put your trough, it may be worth raising it up above ground level. The plants will be easier to see, and you won't spend as much time bent over while you're watering or maintaining your collection. If you're elderly, or disabled in some way, a raised container can be a real godsend.

The container must be frost-resistant, but that's not all. It also needs to have proper drainage if you're going to grow alpines successfully. All alpine troughs need the right number of drainage holes cut to the right size. If a container is 2 ft (60 cm) long, for example, then it should have at least 3-5 holes, each of them with a diameter of ½-1 in (1-2 cm).

When you're filling the container, start by putting some potsherds or similarly shaped stones in the base. This will prevent soil or plant roots from entering and blocking the holes. Then add the so-called drainage layer; this should consist of rough gravel, crushed pumice, clay granules or some similar material (you could also use a mixture of these). The thickness of the drainage layer will depend on the size of your container; it needs to occupy about 25-40 per cent of the available space.

If you're planning to include frost-sensitive perennials or bulbs, then you'll be well advised to cover the sides of the container with an insulating layer of polystyrene tiles. If you put them in against the sides before installing the drainage layer, then

A small alpine collection in a trough made of artificial stone

the pressure of this plus the topsoil above will be enough to push them firmly against the sides. That way you won't need to use any adhesive — although you can, if necessary, use an ordinary plastic adhesive to make absolutely sure that the insulation is properly bonded to the sides.

If the trough is large enough, you can incorporate some suitable stones. There'll only be enough room for a small selection of highly individual stones, but this will be quite enough to create a delightful rock landscape in miniature. The best choice of stone is tufa, especially if it's covered with lots of pits and depressions. Make sure the stones are firmly bedded deep down in the container, so there's no danger of them falling out. Fill the gaps between them with soil, gently pressing it down.

There should be a 1-in (2-cm) gap between the topsoil and the top of the container. The exact composition of the soil will depend on the alpines that you intend to plant. If the trough is made of an alkaline stone such as limestone or calcareous sandstone, then you should use a lime-rich soil and choose lime-loving or lime-tolerant plants.

Conversely, if the trough is made of an acidic stone such as granite or older sandstone, then you should have plants that prefer an acid soil. However, the great majority of alpines for troughs will actually grow in either kind of soil.

A variety of troughs filled with perennials and dwarf shrubs

When you're planning a small alpine collection, it's never easy to decide which plants to select. One option might be to choose plants from a particular region, such as the northern Alps, the Dolomites, the Carpathians or the Himalayas. It's also best to plant shrubs and perennials that have been grown in small pots. The smaller root balls will be easier to accommodate in the limited planting space.

Apart from the various dwarf shrubs and ground-cover perennials, you could also include some suitable bulb or tuber plants. You may be able to train some of the shrubs into interesting bonsai-like forms. And you could also add a few other natural-looking features, such as gnarled sections of old branches or roots, to give the whole display a feeling of age and maturity.

Before starting to plant out, you should first arrange the plants in their pots in the places where you intend to plant them. Use a small dibber or an old kitchen fork to dig out the holes, and wedge the plant roots firmly into the soil. If you don't, they may become exposed as the soil begins to settle, and will then be in danger of drying out.

As soon as you've finished planting out, give the whole area a thorough watering. Bury the plant labels next to the plants so that just a small section of each is visible above the soil. Cover all the remaining areas of exposed soil with a mulch layer about 1 in (2–3 cm) thick. Try to use a mulch made of the same material as the stones in the trough, since this will make the surface area of the trough seem much larger.

Bowls of shrubs can easily be incorporated into the rock garden at a later stage.

Watering

Careful watering is extremely important with trough plants. Unlike a proper rock garden, an alpine trough is subject to additional evaporation through the sides of the container, especially if it's in a raised position. Materials like concrete and reconstituted stone only allow a small amount of moisture loss, but the same can't be said for terracotta or stone troughs, where the limited space for roots is yet another reason for frequent, regular watering. In a warm spot, such as next to a sunlit, south-facing wall, you'll need to water the trough at least once a day.

Watch carefully to see exactly how much water is needed from day to day. Most dwarf shrubs will die if they dry out for only a very short time. At the very least their growth will be affected. With conifers, especially, you simply won't see the danger signs soon enough.

Often the needles won't start to discolour or drop off until several days or even weeks have elapsed.

Apart from direct watering, most trough-dwelling plants like some humidity in the air around them. In hot weather especially, you can raise the ambient humidity by spraying water above the plants.

If you're growing plants that don't like too much moisture, they may be able to survive occasional dry periods. If you have succulent plants, you'll need to cover them up with glass or plastic sheeting during periods of cold or very wet weather. If they're in small bowls or portable containers, you can simply move them to a more sheltered location.

Trough collections

Some British gardeners have turned alpine trough collections into an art form in their own right, creating whole colonies

of troughs of different shapes and sizes, and carefully positioning them in suitable places all round the garden, such as next to pathways, patios or other seating areas.

Making your own stone troughs

Old stone troughs are usually far too expensive for most people to buy, but it's still possible to create your own troughs by carving them from blocks of natural stone.

The best candidates for this kind of treatment are limestone or sandstone blocks left over from old walls or foundations. If you do the job properly, you should end up with a very attractive collection of troughs, at a fraction of the price of a genuine antique.

Start by using a hammer drill to make a long series of holes in the block at ½-1-in (1-2-cm) intervals along the line that will form the outside edge of the planting area. Each hole should be about 1½-2½ in (4-6 cm) deep. Next take a heavy hammer and a sharpened chisel, and chisel out the stone from the drilled holes towards the centre of the block.

Continue to hollow out the stone, layer by layer, until you've cut out a hole the size that you want; 6 in (15 cm) is the minimum depth you'll need for planting purposes.

When you've hollowed the trough to your own satisfaction, turn the block over and drill a series of vertical drainage holes. Start them with a 6-mm or 8-mm masonry drill, then use a much bigger drill to finish off the job.

When you're working with masonry tools you should always wear suitable protective gloves and boots, and also a visor to shield your eyes. You should always check to make sure that there's no one else in the general vicinity who could be injured by any flying fragments of stone.

Another way to create your own troughs is to mould them using a mixture of peat, sand, cement and water.

First make an exterior mould out of wood or strong cardboard. Then take the various ingredients and combine them to make up the 'hypertufa' mixture. The best quantities for this are three parts peat to two parts sand to three parts cement. Add water until you get the right cement-like consistency, and finally pour the mixture into the mould, placing a polystyrene block in the centre to create the hollow section for the planting area.

Leave the mould for five days to a week, then carefully remove it from the trough. Now roughen up the smooth surface with a wire brush, and leave the container to harden up for at least a month before you actually use it.

Troughs made of this peaty mixture are quickly colonised by mosses, lichens and algae. In time they will be difficult to distinguish from troughs that have been cut from natural stone.

Even in such a small space, these tiny alpine plants don't look in the least bit crowded.

Plants for troughs and old sinks

Achillea clavennae
rock cress
Arabis bryoides
sandwort
Arenaria pinifolia
Armeria caespitosa
Artemisia caucasica
Campanula tommassinana
Cardunculus rhaponticoides
alpine pink
Dianthus alpinus
whitlow grass
Draba bruniifolia
fleabane
Erigeron compositus
Erodium chrysanthum
Helichrysum milfordiae
edelweiss
Leontopodium kurilense
alpine marguerite
Leucanthemopsis alpina
flax
Linum campanulatum
Minuartia juniperina
Origanum amanum
Physoplexis comosa
auricula
Primula auricula
Saxifraga crustata
S. squarrosa
cobweb houseleek
Sempervivum arachnoideum

The main rock-garden societies

Alpine Garden Society, AGS Centre, Avon Bank, Pershore, Worcs WR10 3JP

Scottish Rock Garden Club, 21 Merchiston Park, Edinburgh EH10 4PW

Index